# Mind Your Metaphors

*A Critique of Language in
the Bishops' Pastoral Letters
on the Role of Women*

**Maureen Aggeler, RSCJ**

*Paulist Press
New York Mahwah*

Copyright © 1991 by Maureen Aggeler

All rights reserved. No part of this book may be reproduced or transmitted in any form or by any means, electronic or mechanical, including photocopying, recording or by any information storage and retrieval system without permission in writing from the Publisher.

Library of Congress Cataloging-in-Publication Data

Aggeler, Maureen, 1938–
    Mind your metaphors: a critique of language in the bishops' pastoral letters on the role of women/Maureen Aggeler.
      p.  cm.
   Includes bibliographical references.
   ISBN 0-8091-3151-X
    1. Women in the Catholic Church—United States. 2. Catholic Church—United States—Pastoral letters and charges.  3. Catholic Church—United States—Bishops. 4. Catholic Church—Doctrines.  5. Woman (Christian theology)  I. Title:
BX1407.W65A44   1990
282'.082—dc20                                      90-21998
                                                                         CIP

Published by Paulist Press
997 Macarthur Boulevard
Mahwah, New Jersey 07430

Printed and bound in the
United States of America

# Contents

| | |
|---|---|
| *Foreword* | 1 |
| *Introduction* | 5 |
| **1. *A Century of Struggle for Women*** | **17** |
| From 1900 Until Vatican II | 21 |
| From Vatican II Until 1978 | 32 |
| **2. *Metaphors in the Pastorals*** | **47** |
| I. Women and Culture | 53 |
| II. Women and the Church | 66 |
| III. Women and Men | 79 |
| IV. Conversion and Reconciliation | 90 |
| **3. *Toward a New Vision of Church*** | **99** |
| The Church's View of Women: Cardinal Gibbons to Pope Paul VI | 101 |
| The Church's View of Women Today | 108 |
| The First Level: "Prisoners of a Culture" | 109 |
| The Second Level: "New Models of Participation" | 112 |
| The Third Level: "A New Version of Church" | 114 |
| Imagining the Future | 118 |
| *Afterword* | 125 |
| **Exhibits** | |
| A. Bishops' Pastoral Letters 1974–1987 | 127 |

B. Responses of Eleven Bishops to the
    Survey ........................ 128

Table 1—Women and Culture ......... 130
Table 2—Women and the Church ...... 136
Table 3—Women and Men ............ 141
Table 4—Conversion and
    Reconciliation ............... 145

## *Foreword*

This book is the result of a variety of personal experiences in the church as well as of questions about its persistent double message to women. My consciousness was raised in the early 1970s when I studied for the Master of Divinity degree in Berkeley and learned the stories of Episcopal women who struggled to follow their call to ordination. My questions deepened with the experience of the first Ordination Conference in Detroit, 1975, when the quality of speakers and presentations energized an already vibrant community of women to action. Pained and angered by official church response to the movement toward mutuality and full participation of women, I continued my quest in a variety of ecumenical groups and throughout seven years of congregational leadership. In the 1980s, serving on the Bishops' National Advisory Council (NAC), I discovered that active church leaders all over the country sought equitable treatment of women but that groups had not consolidated and opinions about "how far the church should go" varied. Through the NAC, I came to respect the bishops themselves for the extensive agenda with which they dealt, their awareness of the serious responsibility they have toward all the people of God, and their commitment to a collegial process in developing their pastoral letters.

In 1985, at the close of International Women's Year Decade in Nairobi, Kenya, I shared with Catholic women from all over the world who gathered to discuss their concerns and the response of the church. I saw that my questions were not conditioned by my being an American; they were the same for Africans, Asians, Europeans, and South Americans. That same year, I heard Gregory Baum state that the North American bishops had accepted the woman's question as a justice issue; one had only to read their pastoral letters to see that this new consciousness was in the mind of the church—and, he theorized, would not go away. Professor Baum also reiterated his theory that the positive, progressive statements from church hierarchy need to be reinforced. They should be reminded of what they have said and what the People of God expect as a result. I wondered to what extent the bishops had heard women's questions and their desire for full participation. It occurred to me that there might be evidence of a paradigm shift in the U.S. Roman Catholic Bishops' pastoral letters, written over a period of fourteen years, a shift which could indicate that the church is on the brink of major change.

The bishops wrote their letters in response to women who urged that their concerns be addressed, and they invited our response in turn. Aware of the inherent contradiction in the circumstance of male ecclesiastics writing about women, a contradiction that is structural and not personal, I also heard the call to dialogue. Committed to change within the structure, I undertook this study of the twelve pastoral letters inspired by the renewed church's insistence that more radical change be wrought.

In my study, I struggled with different ways to get into the real messages of the pastorals as a unit. The play of metaphoric invention and imagination at first intrigued me, then captured my attention. I decided to listen to the language of metaphor as an essential key to interpretation and then to decipher the metaphors as one would a code in order to grasp the worldview of the authors. I applied Thomas Kuhn's theory of paradigm shift to discover whether the metaphors revealed an insight about the revolutionary change needed in the structures to accommodate women's full participation. As the church images such future realities as women priests and bishops, shared decisions and policy-making, a new language will be developed. A change in consciousness will be revealed. The new images, symbols, and metaphors will help bring about the paradigm shift.

This book is *not* a commentary on the American Catholic Bishops' Pastoral addressing women's concerns. The widespread consultation process which formed the basis of their letter coincided with the beginnings of my research. I finished my work before the first draft of the bishops' pastoral was circulated. It is my hope that this study will contribute to the discussion and dialogue necessary to move us forward in our search for a new way to be church—one that calls forth the full humanity of both women and men. This book is addressed to all the People of God, although I am convinced that it is women who are key to the structural change that must take place in our church. It is for us to describe our experience as church and our vision of what the church of equal partners will look like. It is for us to refuse the hierarchical construction of the relationship between male and female in its specific contexts and choose the way of mutuality.

I wish to thank warmly many friends and colleagues for their assistance and support. Margaret Brennan, Catherine Lacey, and Mary Ellen Sheehan were encouraging mentors in the early stage of my research. Mary Helen Washington, at once my most demanding and supportive critic, helped me clarify what I wanted to say and gave me the benefit of her editorial skills. Moni McIntyre, Cora Twohig Moengongango, and my RSCJ communities in Boston and Toronto offered unfailing interest and creative comments. Barbara Hope, Anne Dyer, Maribeth Tobin, Elizabeth O'Connor kept a steady interest in my revisions. I am particularly grateful to Jean Bartunek, Mary Hunt, and Madeleine Sophie Cooney who read the manuscript and gave invaluable advice and suggestions in preparing it for publication. Finally, I wish to dedicate this book to my mother, Jane McGrath Aggeler, and my sisters, Anne, Sheila and Janet—each of them, faithful women of the church.

## *Introduction*

When the National Council of Catholic Bishops (NCCB) voted at their November 1983 meeting to write a pastoral letter on women, the decision came out of a twenty year history of grappling with the "woman question." Since Vatican Council II, eleven pastoral letters on women had been addressed to local U.S. dioceses. A twelfth letter followed, in 1987. Their issuance from 1974 to 1987 constitutes an important historical precedent for the NCCB 1988 publication of "Partners in Redemption." They witness to the fact that women's long acceptance of a subservient role has given way to a sacred and serious search for full expression of their gifts within the church understood as the people of God. What do the twelve letters tell us about this search—and about the face of the church in the future?

At the outset, there must be acknowledgement of the fact that women wrote the basic text of several pastorals studied in this book. Nevertheless, the responsibility for the redaction of texts rests with the bishops. Because the pastorals are issued in their name, the insights, theology, and language may be attributed to them. It is also important to note that in the process of examining the challenges and vision presented by a renewed church, some of the hierarchy have changed their perspective and now acknowledge that sexism is an ecclesial problem, not women's problem.

Although markedly different, the twelve letters have some elements in common. They all base their remarks on the teaching of Vatican II about the essential dignity of the human person (*Gaudium et Spes* 29) and on an interpretation of Jesus' relationship with women. They acknowledge injustices suffered by women in society and in the church, and they assert that women's growth and dignity are hampered by discrimination. They offer encouragement for and recognition of women's faithful witness throughout the centuries. They recognize and respond to the need for affirmative action in church hiring practices.

They call for reconciliation, at times proposing a church service to formalize it. Finally, many of them intimate that the future of women's ministry is yet to be determined.

A chronological survey of the pastorals indicates the nationwide sweep of interest in women's role in the church, from small dioceses to large archdioceses. (See Exhibit A for a chronological listing of the bishops' letters.) Four individual bishops, Leo T. Maher of San Diego (August 1974), Carrol T. Dozier of Memphis (January 1975), Charles A. Buswell of Pueblo (December 1975), and William D. Borders of Baltimore (August 1977) addressed the people of their dioceses from various perspectives on the topic of women in the church. Meanwhile, the Minnesota bishops (Archbishop John B. Roach of St. Paul and Minneapolis; Bishop Paul E. Anderson of Duluth; Bishop Victor H. Balke of Crookston; Bishop Raymond A. Lucker of New Ulm; Bishop George H. Speltz of St. Cloud; Bishop Loras J. Watters of Winona; and Auxiliary Bishop John F. Kinney of St. Paul and Minneapolis) had commissioned a task force to write a pastoral in their name. Differences in style and in theological presentation, however, led the Minnesota bishops to write a statement of their own; the two statements were published together in one booklet (March 1979). Next, three more individual bishops addressed their local churches: Archbishop Raymond G. Hunthausen of Seattle (April 1980), Archbishop Peter L. Gerety of Newark (February 1981), and John S. Cummins of Oakland (October 1981). Shortly afterward, two of the Minnesota bishops, Balke and Lucker, issued their own statement on women in the church to their dioceses (October 1981). Several months later, Bishop Matthew H. Clark published a long and fully developed theological pastoral on women to the Rochester diocese (April 1982). The lengthiest document treated in this study is the published report of the Task Force on Women in the Church commissioned by Archbishop Rembert G. Weakland, OSB, for the church in southeast Wisconsin, with an introductory statement by the archbishop (November 1982). The twelfth and final

## Introduction 7

pastoral which preceded the first draft of the NCCB letter (1988) addressed to the people of Los Angeles by Archbishop Roger Mahony (August 1987).

There are many curious and engaging details which surround the development of the twelve pastorals in the local churches. Except for Bishop Dozier, who died before this book was written, each of the bishops obligingly answered a short survey which indicated: (1) his intention in writing the pastoral, (2) the source of inspiration for writing the letter, (3) the process by which the letter was developed, and (4) what happened in his diocese as a result of the pastoral letter. (See Exhibit B for a description of common responses to the survey.) From these data, it is clear that most of the letters were written to encourage women to participate more fully in the total mission and life of the church, and in many cases committees or commissions were mandated to study the issues further and develop practical ways to assist women in the church. The impetus for the letters generally came from women.

Archbishop Borders stated that his pastoral letter "was written out of both the promptings of grass roots Catholics in Baltimore and [his] own thoughts on the matter." In Oakland, the members of the Senate Committee on Women in Ministry suggested that Bishop Cummins write a pastoral letter. In Crookston, a group called "Bread and Roses" asked Bishop Balke to write a pastoral letter and supplied him with the resource material; Bishop Lucker of New Ulm made some suggestions for writing the final draft and co-issued it. Sister Margaret Ellen Traxler, a long-time friend of Bishop Dozier, reported that his letter came in response to the request of numerous women who felt that he understood their issues. Bishop Buswell listened to the women religious in the Pueblo diocese who advocated the idea of affirmative action, although his commitment to promote women's position in the church pre-dated his pastoral. Archbishop Hunthausen acknowledged that the letter was written out of his own inspiration and the encouragement of women in his archdiocese.

In the church in Minnesota, according to Archbishop Roach of Saint Paul and Minneapolis, the letter was, "through all the years of its development, a product both of the bishops' concern and the urging of grass roots Catholics." Bishop Clark consulted with people in Rochester regarding their concerns, the need for and timing of a pastoral on women, but the letter was written out of his own inspiration. Archbishop Gerety of Newark wrote a pastoral letter "because of [his] feeling that the time had come for leadership on this issue in our archdiocese." He had reached this conclusion "as a result of listening to many of [his] people expressing . . . their desire that this issue of the position of women be listed as an urgent priority for the church." In Milwaukee, a Task Force to study the concerns of women was suggested by the archdiocesan pastoral council and priests' council, Archbishop Weakland wrote, because "we felt that we should find out what our people were really thinking." Bishop Maher of San Diego, whose letter preceded the others, reported that his pastoral "was entirely of my own inspiration." Finally, Archbishop Mahony wrote his letter as a follow-up to a process initiated by his predecessor, Cardinal Manning, in order "to respond directly and clearly to the issues and concerns raised in [the] hearing process."

From this sketch we can conclude that the pastoral letters did not arise from any single source. They resulted from much discussion, the gathering of preliminary materials, and questioning of women about their experience and insights. Most (especially the last four pastorals written by Bishops Balke and Lucker, Clark, Mahony, and the task force in Milwaukee) involved the laity, women and men also, a collaboration that suggests the increasing freedom and desire to contribute to the affairs of the church. In fact, the powerful "listening sessions," which came to be incorporated in the Task Force Report in Milwaukee, became the verbatim material of the letter. Sister Rita Burns, a member of the task force, describes how the report was written:

> I recall vividly the task force's first meeting after all the listening sessions had taken place. It was time to decide what to do about a report. The group's cynics were ready to abandon the whole project, saying that nothing would come of it anyway. Those with more pleasant personalities were ready to report what the women had said but they suggested that we couldn't really say it like it was said to us. They thought we needed to tone it down a bit; the disillusionment and alienation and anger were just too raw. After all, church-related documents are almost always happy talk—ideals, hopes, and promises. The die-hards among us (those I would call the "pure in heart") won out. The task force agreed to say what was said in all its rawness.[1]

Archbishop Weakland chose to publish the report in its entirety; he wrote the introduction. For the purposes of this study, the source of the quoted material from the pastoral will be designated either as Weakland's introduction or the text of the report.

Apparently no bishop simply sat at his desk and wrote a pastoral letter. The bishops variously reported that dialogue, interviews, informal meetings, ongoing discussions, surveys by task forces, and hearings helped in the development of the pastorals. In several dioceses, for example San Diego and Newark, select women's committees were asked to advise the bishops and in fact contributed much to the final document. Bishop Maher (San Diego) is the only bishop who acknowledged by name the woman (Mrs. Beryl Newman) and committee (The Rights and Dignity of Women) who contributed to the pastoral. In the archdiocese of Saint Paul and Minneapolis, a task force on the role

---

[1] Rita Burns, "Breaking the Grand Silence: a diocesan process." Unpublished paper presented at the National Conference on Women in the Church, Washington, D.C., October 1987.

of women which functioned at the time the pastoral was developed was responsible for an extensive survey which gave issue to a two-part report in 1977 and 1978. The report included numerous and far-reaching recommendations which later formed the basis of the Plan of Action issued by Archbishop Roach. The importance of collegiality in this period of history is revealed in the process of developing the pastoral letters.

In most dioceses the process itself stirred new interest in women's issues. The interest increased with the publication of the letters, which often resulted in some concrete action, such as the development of affirmative action hiring procedures. In both Seattle and Saint Paul-Minneapolis, a women's commission was formed. In Crookston, a designated task force met with parish councils and sought ways to create a climate for the implementation of the pastoral letter. In Rochester, the task force which had served as a consultative body to Bishop Clark during the writing of the pastoral continued to work for more than a year. Members encouraged discussion and implementation of the sixteen courses of action spelled out in the letter and then published a lengthy report of the results compiled from local church imput. In Newark, a Priests' Senate Task Force studied the pastoral and made eight recommendations. These recognized the need for discussion of the interaction of men and women in ministry, and concluded with this forward-looking statement:

> The existing Church law leaves women's ministry limited and incomplete. Women's ordination to the diaconate and the priesthood certainly should be an available option to women responding to God's individual call. The whole body of the Church is truly served less [by] being ministered to solely by males. The male priesthood itself shares in this limitation. For these reasons, we look forward to sincere, substantial dialogue on every level concerning this issue. Our hope is that the Church of

Newark assume leadership in this openness and
be a model of this dialogue.[2]

In Baltimore, dialogue continued after the issuance of the pastoral, even up to the spring of 1987, when a women's committee approached the archbishop with further recommendations. In Pueblo, a definite raising of consciousness occurred because of the pastoral. Within twelve to eighteen months of its issuance, "four out of eleven diocesan agencies were headed by women."

Two dioceses reported minimal activity. In Oakland, the response was "difficult to measure"; the letter seemed to encourage "both men and women who wanted to promote women's roles in ministry and address justice issues." In San Diego, Bishop Maher reported that the letter "made the women recognize their importance in the local church and manifested the concern of the bishop for them."

Sizes of the pastorals range from leaflet-size (Hunthausen and Buswell) to an artistically designed twelve-page tabloid newspaper (Clark). Two are medium-size pamphlets (Minnesota Bishops Balke and Lucker). Most are small pamphlets (Maher, Dozier, Borders, Cummins). One was simultaneously published in two languages, Italian and English, in magazine size (Gerety). In Los Angeles, the four-page tabloid with pictures (some in color) of local women in leadership roles was an insert in the weekly archdiocesan newspaper (Mahony). The southeast Wisconsin Task Force report, a twelve-page tabloid paper, is the longest of the documents. Many of these letters were subsequently published in *Origins*.

Notably, the perspective each bishop takes in developing his pastoral differs according to the bishop's own outlook and his experience of the needs of his local church. This is signified in both the title and the theme of each

---

[2] Priests' Senate Task Force Report on Women (Recommendations to Archbishop Peter L. Gerety), Newark, New Jersey, 1981.

pastoral. Bishop Maher's statement, comprehensive in scope, is situated in the global community: "Women in the New World." The language of Bishop Dozier's letter, "Woman: intrepid and loving," is characteristically informal and intuitive, as he explores where "the journey toward wholeness" will lead us. Bishop Buswell's clear purpose, to bring the principles of affirmative action into the structures of the local church, shaped his letter, "Ecclesial Affirmative Action." Archbishop Borders' letter, "Women in the Church," contains an informal beginning and ending which frame an otherwise doctrinal statement; it also includes a clear commitment to advocate for advancing women's place in the church. The Minnesota bishops issued "Woman: Pastoral Reflections," which combines a practical statement with a justice orientation (by the task force) with a shorter section of theological reflections (by the bishops) on the various roles of woman in the family, in society, and in the church. Archbishop Hunthausen's "Pastoral Statement on Women" begins and ends with a reference to the example of St. Catherine of Siena, "known to have urged obedience to legal church authority, while at the same time challenging popes to face the structural issues of their day."

Archbishop Gerety's pastoral "Women in the Church" might be read as a theological treatise on the church, with an effort to situate women's role within the traditional church structures. Bishop Cummins' statement on "Women in Ministry" affirms the present ministry of women in the Oakland diocese and includes recommendations and a call to action. Bishop Balke's and Bishop Lucker's pastoral, "Male and Female God Created Them," explores the roots and pervasiveness of sexism, contrasts society's denigration of women with Jesus' treatment of women, and includes a model examination of conscience about one's attitudes and pastoral practices with regard to women. "The Fire in the Thornbush," issued by Bishop Clark, explores a wide range of topics in ninety-three paragraphs: Mary; women's history in the church; the need for reconciliation; women's spirituality and mission today; the church as prophet, priest and shepherd; the future.

The Task Force Report of the "listening sessions" in the church in southeast Wisconsin contains a description of the task force, the context of the sessions, and a profile of the participants; it gives detailed accounts of the women's reported experiences and areas of need in the archdiocese, and it concludes with numerous concrete recommendations. Finally, Archbishop Mahony entitled his pastoral "Just as the Women Said" by way of suggesting that "all too often in our Christian history men have been slow to listen to what women have been saying." He acknowledges the gifts women bring to the church of Los Angeles and reflects at length on two practical areas where immediate progress can occur: attention must be paid to the use of inclusive language and to the placement of women in policy formation and decision-making levels within the church.

The variety of purposes and themes reveals that the topic of women in the church is complex; it can be validly and appropriately approached from many different perspectives. It seems likely that each bishop's experience of women, the education and background which he brought to the composition of his letter, and the input from those whom he chose to consult, were all formative in shaping his letter's purpose, theme, and theological reflection. Yet, the resulting variety of pastorals, written in such different styles and addressing needs particular to the local churches, can be viewed as a whole, much the way we approach scripture with its multiformity of texts, writing styles, and plurality of authors. Taken together as a composite, the pastorals might be said to reflect a summary view of the state of the "woman question" in the U.S. hierarchical church from 1974 to 1987. In this book they will be considered as a unit.

These twelve letters are clearly the outcome of the U.S. church in renewal since the Second Vatican Council. Situated mid-century in a period when the women's movement was gaining undeniable momentum, the council not only debated the great issues of our times but saw the need to affirm each person's dignity and the essential equality of men and women. Momentous change followed the council, including the effects of women's heightened sense of full personhood and a moral and social responsibility that propelled them into the public sector, heretofore reserved for men. The church also witnessed the expression of women's fuller consciousness in feminist theology, which unmasked the deep sexual bias in church teaching and practice.

Today, more than twenty-five years since Vatican Council II and after a century of ferment and struggle to gain equal rights in society, many women continue to challenge the structures which persist in allowing them only a subordinate role in the church. With ever greater insistence, women, and men also, now call for changes which will lead to full equality of women in the church. Have the U.S. bishops heard the challenge? The question is important because of the primary teaching role of the bishops in their local churches; it is urgent because of the numbers of women whose experience of alienation in the church has led them to leave it.

Those bishops who wrote pastoral letters to their local churches have recognized the need for new ways of talking about and promoting women's dignity and rights as baptized members of the church. The letters have the authority of the local bishop for his diocese and are in the tradition of the apostle Paul, who often used this effective teaching tool. In addition to their teaching role, the bishops have responsibility for the social unity of the church. They shape the Catholic tradition for the future as they give voice to the community's faith and belief and watch over its worship. Their letters on women potentially affect the whole faith community who may rightly ask: Will this teaching apply the values of the prevailing system or will the bishops risk promoting liberating policies and practices that can truly humanize our church? Can this body of literature be said to represent a new vision?

This book explores the pastoral letters in order to investigate the extent to which they open the way to a new vision of church, where equality is called for on all levels. To discover this, a hermeneutic is employed which will help discover an analogy between the historical situation of the past and the practice and statement linked to it, and the present historical situation and the question to which it gives rise.

It is proposed in this book that the bishops' creation and use of metaphors indicate their social construction of reality. The metaphor is a conceptual construct, an image, which organizes and puts limits on experience. With a metaphor, a speaker develops connotations and can create new contextual meaning. It is not surprising that in the pastoral letters, metaphor thrives—particularly in the interpretative aspect of women's experience. By focusing on metaphor in a content analysis of the pastoral letters, we may observe the bishops' dynamics of thought.

As the bishops depict their world and construe their experience in the letters, their chosen metaphors are prime indicators of their meaning. In order to understand this meaning, the methodology employed here is as follows. First, the metaphors found in the letters are compiled and then classified in distinct categories. The metaphors are "unpacked" and interpreted as a reflection of the basic worldview of the authors. Questions are raised about meaning, and an assessment is made of the contribution of the pastorals to the discussion of women and the church in this period of history.

The first chapter establishes an historical context for the pastorals. It explores some relevant church teachings from 1911 to 1978 as they relate to women. The material is divided into two main sections, separated by Vatican Council II which marked the beginning of a shift in the church's articulation of its understanding of women as persons and as members of the church. While it is but a brief survey of the pertinent material, this chapter provides some necessary background for understanding the tradition from which these pastoral letters emerge.

The second chapter presents an exposition of the content of the pastorals through a study of the metaphors. For each of the four categories, a table of metaphors has been developed (see pp. 130ff). The tables include a listing of metaphorical statements by topic:

Table 1: Women and Culture
Table 2: Women and the Church
Table 3: Women and Men
Table 4: Conversion and Reconciliation

The interpretation of their meaning emerges out of my own horizon of understanding. In addition, questions are raised about the theological insights these metaphors reveal.

It is proposed in the third chapter that the bishops' metaphorical constructions actually serve as paradigms and can be taken as indices for the bishops' thinking as a group. Although it is incomplete, their vision of women's role in the contemporary church stands in sharp contrast to the ecclesiological documentation on women which appeared during the first half of this century. Their language (and specifically their metaphors) shows the extent of the dramatic shift in thinking about women which was already incipient in the documents of Vatican II. Conclusions are drawn about the degree to which the bishops critique present church structures and help us envision a paradigm of church which will accommodate our new understanding of personhood, equality, and mutuality.

# Chapter 1

# A Century of Struggle for Women

Women and the church have seldom had a trouble-free association—their tug and pull is witnessed throughout art, philosophy, literature, and history. Since the time of Jesus, when his disciples "were greatly surprised to find him talking with a woman," the making of *church* has been a male prerogative:

> But none of them said to her, "What do you want?" or asked him, "Why are you talking with her?" (Jn 4:27).

Nevertheless, since the time of Jesus, women have been following him, using "their own resources to help [him] and his disciples" (Lk 8:3).

In recent times, a new context has developed for talking about women and the church; it is the "second wave" of the women's movement which converges with the changes wrought by Vatican Council II. We are on the verge of a painful but urgent transformation. Women are struggling to free themselves from an inferior status in the social, political, and intellectual spheres. The renewed church is struggling for relevance in a society where women have successfully broken boundaries. As in Jesus' time, women in the church have neither a forum nor ecclesiastical power to say what they want; it is for the bishops to surmise and interpret women's desires. Twelve pastoral letters, issued since 1974, represent their effort to situate women's role in today's church in light of the new context.

Only recently have women achieved the kind of solidarity and political will to challenge effectively the symbol system, theological language and methodology, as well as the tradition and structures which have oppressed them. The twelve pastoral letters may be read as a response to that challenge. The question raised in this chapter is: How has the church's position regarding women's role undergone a change in this century?

The intent of this chapter is to explore pertinent official church positions which related to key events for twentieth century women, such as the suffrage movement and passage of the 19th amendment, the introduction of the ERA, and women's increasing participation in the work force during World War I and World War II. The sporadic attempts of women to break out of their inferior status often met with suspicion and hostility, in the secular sphere as well as in the church. However, it is possible to observe a dramatic shift of attitude toward woman which began with the Second Vatican Council and which is evident in the council documents themselves. In the years since then, the renewed church has sought to incorporate within the existing paradigm some of the newly-articulated understandings of women's equal dignity with men.

Because church teaching is made relevant in a specific secular context, it is important first of all to establish society's heritage from nineteenth century teaching about women.

## *The Heritage of Genteel Femininity*

Most nineteenth century American women were not much different from their European counterparts who internalized the values of true womanhood. A cluster of ideas and well-defined standards of behavior formed the cult of domesticity which was to become an integral part of American social ideology. Its force may be observed in the writings of Alexis de Tocqueville who traveled across the continent in the early 1830s. He observed that in the U.S. "the inexorable opinion of the public carefully circumscribes women within the narrow circle of domestic interests and duties and forbids her to step beyond it." In often quoted passages, he related those observations which led him to this conclusion.

In America the independence of woman is irrecoverably lost in the bonds of matrimony. If an unmarried woman is less constrained there than elsewhere, a wife is subjected to stricter obligations. The former makes her father's house an abode of freedom and of pleasure; the latter lives in the home of her husband as if it were a cloister. Yet these two different conditions of life are perhaps not so contrary as may be supposed, and it is natural that American women should pass through the one to arrive at the other.

In no country has such constant care been taken as in America to trace two clearly distinct lines of action for the two sexes and to make them keep pace one with the other, but in two pathways that are always different. American women never manage the outward concerns of the family or conduct a business or take part in political life; nor are they, on the other hand, ever compelled to perform rough labor of the fields or to make any of those laborious efforts which demand the exertion of physical strength.[1]

The literature and art of the period faithfully mirror this picture of constraint: women's carefully regulated life and subjection to men. DeTocqueville traveled at a time when female advice literature warned women against those qualities of assertiveness and resourcefulness which characterized colonial women in earlier times and also frontier women, about whom he did not write. He did, however, capture many women's experience of an increasingly nar-

---

[1] Alexis de Tocqueville, *Democracy in America* (trans. Henry Reeve), revised edition (New York: Collier and Son, 1900), Vol. II, pp. 211, 222.

row world and specialized role. Generally, as their direct relationship to economic productivity lessened, women's assertiveness and independence were muted.

In the decades following deTocqueville's visit, the virtues of piety, purity, submissiveness, and domesticity became enshrined in the Victorian era as an ideology of true womanhood. The proper Christian woman of the nineteenth century prayed regularly, provided an orderly, tranquil environment for husband and children, and guarded her home from the corrosive influences of the world. Her domestic world, sharply segregated from the all-male economic world outside, was her proper sphere. Her dominion in the home, however, always existed in the context of continued subordination:

> The mark of spiritual progress for woman was the complete repression of her feelings. Socialized to deny her desires for self-assertion and power, the model nineteenth century woman accepted that her husband's authority was sanctioned by God, nature and tradition. Thus, even though the cult of domesticity frequently proclaimed the equality of the male and female spheres, in fact—and even in theory—the home over which the wife presided was always seen as ultimately subordinate to male authority.[2]

It must also be noted that the prescribed ideal was not accessible to women of the frontier, slave women, or domestic servants, who had problems and harsh realities of their own. In addition, there were those who escaped the ethic of true womanhood in communitarian societies, re-

---

[2] Barbara J. Harris, *Beyond Her Sphere: Women and the Professions in American History* (Westport, Connecticut: Greenwood Press, 1978), p. 35. See also Rosemary Ruether, "Home and Work," in Walter Burghardt, SJ, ed., *Woman: New Dimensions* (New York: Paulist Press, 1977), pp. 65–80.

form movements, or writing. American Catholic women were among those who upheld the prevailing ideology and also among those who escaped it.[3]

## From 1900 Until Vatican II

Official church teaching on women and their role from 1900 until Vatican II was rooted in Victorian attitudes that enshrined the four "feminine" virtues and the cult of domesticity. The view of womanhood which these attitudes represent was supposedly reinforced by biological differences and grounded in an historical tradition which proclaimed the supremacy of patriarchal structures. Because of woman's biological function in procreation, men assigned them to the home and to their "natural" roles of child-bearing and child-rearing as the nucleus of the family structure. The best way for a woman to exert her power was through a quiet influence on her husband and children. Any deviation from this designated role would surely upset the order of the universe. On the one hand, woman was expected to submit her very being to man; on the other, she was enjoined to preside over the home as a model of purity and goodness apart from the evils of society.

Supported by this prevailing ideology, official church teaching in the early part of this century is not surprising. U.S. bishops were solidly on record against women's suffrage. Their reasons found articulation in the writings and speeches of James Cardinal Gibbons of Baltimore, who was the most outspoken among the hierarchy. In an interview printed in the *New York Globe* on June 22, 1911, he said:

> Woman suffrage? I am surprised that anyone should ask the question. I have but one answer to such a question, and that is that I am unalterably

---

[3] Madonna Kolbenschlag, HM, "The American Woman in Perspective," in *The Challenge of Sisterhood* (South Bend, Indiana: Sir William's Printing Co., 1975), p. 3.

opposed to women's suffrage, always have been, and always will be. . . . Why should a woman lower herself to sordid politics? Why should a woman leave her home and go into the street to play the game of politics? Why should she long to come into contact with men who are her inferiors intellectually and morally? . . . When a woman enters the political arena, she goes outside the sphere for which she was intended. She gains nothing by that journey. On the other hand, she loses the exclusiveness, respect, and dignity to which she is entitled in her home.[4]

This passage indicates the nature of the intensive gender socialization and pyramidal social structure which carried over from the nineteenth century. Two years later the cardinal said: "Equal rights do not imply that both sexes should engage promiscuously in the same pursuits, but that each should discharge those duties which are adapted to its physical constitution."[5] Here, Gibbons seems to be suggesting that women would give an inordinate amount of time to politics if allowed, and that their biological "nature" does not fit them to pursue responsibilities in that arena.

With the passage of the 19th Amendment in 1920, the movement to legalize the dissemination of birth control in-

---

[4] *The New York Globe*, June 22, 1911. Cited in Antoinette Iadarola, "The American Catholic Bishops and Woman," in Yvonne Haddad and Ellison Findly, eds., *Women, Religion and Social Change* (New York: Suny Press, 1985), p. 460. I am greatly indebted to Iadarola for insights and documentation of episcopal writing on women in the early part of this century.

[5] Quotation from a letter to the Maryland Association Opposed to Woman Suffrage. Cited in Iadarola, p. 461. Iadarola observes elsewhere that "the characteristics of women were seen simultaneously as unchangeably rooted in woman's biological 'nature' and yet something that would be 'lost' instantly if she stepped out of her designated 'place'" (p. 458).

formation, and the introduction of the ERA within a decade, the definition of woman's place was hotly debated in many sectors—among psychiatrists, sociologists, politicians, and, of course, churchmen. The implications of these events for women's liberation may have been intuitively grasped by observers of cultural change, but their far-reaching effects would only be realized some four decades later.

When women achieved their right to vote, the views of the Catholic clergy toward women shifted slightly; they seemed to go along with women's vote—but not as a citizen's right. In a 1919 pastoral, the bishops foresaw the passage of the Amendment and adjusted their teaching. But they still did not allow Catholic women the right as human beings to participate in the democratic process; they only conceded that women's vote was needed to "reach the hearts of men and take away their bitterness," and to balance the vote of other women who sought reforms seen as threatening to the home and family.[6]

In a second 1919 pastoral, "Bishops' Program of Social Reconstruction," a forward-looking social justice agenda in the area of labor reform was advanced. The bishops devoted a whole section of this pastoral to the phenomenon of "Women War Workers," spelling out in capsule form the American Catholic Church's future direction in regard to women.[7] The large number of women who had replaced men in the work force during the war years created a problem of readjustment, not only for the men returning to civilian work but for the women in the marketplace who would be displaced. The bishops' consistent message, that women's place is in the home, is implicit in the "general principles" they delineated. The first one stated that "No female worker should remain in any occupation that is

---

[6] "Pastoral Letter of 1919," in *Our Bishops Speak*, 1919–1951, ed. Raphael Huber (Milwaukee: Bruce Publishing Company, 1952), p. 46.

[7] *Our Bishops Speak*, pp. 243–60.

harmful to health or morals" and included such occupations as streetcar conductor, streetcar guard, and locomotive cleaner. Another "general principle" was the admonition "that the proportion of women in industry ought to be kept within the smallest practical limits." The message was clear: women were to return to the home.[8] With the introduction of the ERA in 1923, however, a new threat came to the bishops' position.

By 1924, the National Council of Catholic Women was ready to take an official stand against the Equal Rights Amendment. At their annual convention in St. Louis, the membership passed a resolution protesting its passage "because of the jeopardy in which it places the interests of women." The League of Women Voters and The Women's Bureau of the U.S. Department of Labor supported their position.[9]

Lively debates ensued over the next decade, with the question of protective legislation becoming the crux of the argument. The differences centered on opposing conceptions of female equality. Feminists contended that women and men were alike in their principal attributes and that women's freedom meant achieving identity and equality with men in all areas of life regulated by the law. On the other side, reformers believed that there were physical and psychological differences between men and women which would not allow women to compete on an equal basis with men. This group advocated special labor laws to preserve the rights of the "weaker sex." The perceived need for protective legislation was further reinforced by an attitude toward women as transient workers unlikely to organize themselves.[10] Father John A. Ryan, head of the Social

---

[8] See Rosemary Ruether, *Home and Work*. Ruether discusses "the ethical split between 'moral man' (private man) and 'immoral society' (public man)" in relation to work and home, masculine and feminine, p. 78.

[9] Iadarola, "The American Catholic Bishops and Woman," p. 463.

[10] Iadarola, p. 464.

Welfare Department of the National Catholic Welfare Council, was among those who held this view and fought for the defeat of the ERA.[11]

Discussion about woman's "place" continued on all levels, in society and within the church. In 1930, Pius XI wrote an encyclical, *Casti Connubii,* in which he described woman's efforts to achieve equality as debasing and unnatural. In this encyclical on marriage he invoked the traditional notion that the wife was "the heart of the home," the husband, "the head." His successor went further. Pius XII asserted that "The heroism of motherhood is the pride and glory of the Christian wife" and that "every woman is called to be a mother, mother in the physical sense or mother in a sense more spiritual and more exalted, yet real, nonetheless." In the Pauline tradition, he exhorted women to continue to be submissive to their husbands' authority and he warned: "Many voices will suggest rather a proud autonomy; they will repeat that you are in every respect the equal of your husband, and in many respects his superior. Do not react like Eve to these lying, tempting, deceitful voices."[12]

In contrast to such strong exhortations to women to remain in the home, the labor shortage during World War II called women back to the workplace. Propaganda for the employment of women was everywhere:

> To this task, the molders of public opinion in newspapers, magazines, and radio turned their considerable power. They created *Rosie the Riveter,* who became the lauded symbol of the woman temporarily at work. In all the media,

---

[11] Iadarola, p. 464. See pp. 462–464 for an indication of Ryan's wide influence on official church opinion.

[12] Pius XI, *Casti Connubii,* 1930, in *The Woman in the Modern World: Papal Teachings,* eds., Benedictine Monks of Solesmes (Boston: St. Paul Editions, 1959), pp. 37–38, and in the same collection, Pius XII, "To All Italian Women," October 1945, p. 131, and "To All Newly Weds," September 1941, pp. 68–69. Cited in Iadarola, p. 473.

women at work were pictured and praised, and the woman who did not at least raise a 'victory garden' or work as a volunteer for the Red Cross was made to feel as guilty as the working woman had been made to feel in times past. Even the movies joined in. As part of their effort to bolster national morale, moviemakers churned out a steady stream of pro-allied propaganda films. In these films, the wife or sweetheart who stayed behind and went to work in a regular job or for an agency like the USO became as familiar a figure as the valiant soldier-lover for whom she waited.[13]

The bishops, however, continued with their admonishments. One contended that "we shall have lost the war, if we lose the home" and others stated their fear of woman's mind and heart being turned "away from the home, thereby depriving the family, State and church of her proper contributions to the common welfare."[14] The Vatican, in addition to advising women to return to the home and devote themselves to the duties of motherhood, defined the dogma of the assumption in 1950. Four years later the pope proclaimed a Marian year. The church sought many ways to emphasize the spiritual nature of women's marginalization from society, effectively privatizing their worth and dignity.

Cutbacks among women workers, particularly in industry, began as soon as peace was declared. In post-war years, many female factory workers were displaced in the

---

[13] Lois Banner, *Women in Modern America: A brief history.* Second edition (San Diego: Harcourt Brace Jovanovich, 1984), p. 219. Banner states that the proportion of women in the labor force increased from 25 percent in 1940 to 36 percent in 1945 (p. 219). She also cites a Women's Bureau study in 1944 which showed that 90 percent of the women who had worked throughout the war wanted to continue in their jobs (p. 223).

[14] Both in Huber, *Our Bishops Speak,* pp. 112 and 119.

labor force. These women likely became the suburban housewives of the 1950s, and shortly afterward the subject matter for Betty Friedan's research on "the problem with no name." Their aspirations, like those of the women before them, coexisted with harsh and bitter social realities which provoked difficult political struggles. However, they are the ones who gave birth to the new forms of political action and cooperation which marked the 1960s. Changes in women's personality and economic and family position shaped the nature of the new social movement, which burst into life again after a hiatus of over four decades.

The neat splits of the pre-Vatican II church (the church and the world, the sacred and the secular, laity and religious) were to give way to an inclusive ecclesiology and mandate for social change. At the end of the 1950s, Pope John XXIII summoned a Vatican Council to open "the windows of the church and let in the fresh air." A reform-minded era began, even as sharp differences of opinion were aired. Scholars and clerics and lay people alike sought to read the "signs of the times," to forge new approaches to problems as they sought to remain authentically faithful to the prior tradition. The documents proceeding from Vatican II (September 1963–December 1965) asked the church to address the serious problems of the world. The newly-emphasized dignity and equality of all persons became the foundational principle in subsequent social documents of the church.

During the 1960s in North America, an unprecedented number of women scholars in the fields of philosophy, religion, art, history, literature and anthropology began to write and publish. The volume and substance of their work gradually affected public attitudes toward women. Male assumptions and interpretive biases were challenged, as in Valerie Saiving's landmark essay in feminist theology, where she introduced the fact that the particulars of a theologian's experience as male or female have a direct bearing on his/her stance: "I propose to criticize," she announced, "from the viewpoint of feminine experience, the estimate of the human situation made by certain contemporary theologians."[15]

In the same period, official church teaching continued to reflect traditional attitudes toward the role of women. For example, in his much read and admired encyclical, *Pacem in Terris* (1963), Pope John XXIII stated, "Women have the right to working conditions in accordance with their requirements and their duties as wives and mothers" (n. 19). Note that the right is stated and at once qualified so as to assure women's "special place." While such ambiguity is echoed in subsequent council documents, so is the originality of the pope's integration of the "signs of the times" with a new anthropology, evident in this passage from *Pacem in Terris:*

> . . . it is obvious to everyone that women are now taking part in public life. This is happening more rapidly perhaps in nations of Christian civilization and more slowly, but broadly, among peoples who have inherited other traditions and cultures. Since women are becoming more conscious of their human dignity, they will not tolerate being treated as mere material instruments, but demand rights befitting a human person both in domestic and public life (n. 41).

The significance of this statement lies in the pope's recognition of something new occurring in human consciousness, one of the "signs of the times" which invite the church to discover an appropriate place for women in church life. Thus, the pope laid the cornerstone for the

---

[15] Valerie Saiving, "The Human Situation: A Feminine View," in Carol P. Christ and Judith Plaskow, eds. *Womanspirit Rising* (San Francisco: Harper and Row, 1979), pp. 25–42. First published in *Journal of Religion* 40 (April 1960), pp. 100–112.

exploration of woman's role in the era of aggiornamento which followed.[16]

The year 1963 proved to be a landmark in the history of American women especially. Betty Friedan's book *The Feminine Mystique* was the ideological keynote and call for action of the new feminism. In her study, Friedan sought to delineate "the problem that has no name" suffered by "the happy housewife heroine." She contended that women were victimized by a "feminine mystique" which prevailed in society—an insistence that woman's happiness lay in fulfilling the role of wife and mother. Friedan offered "a new life plan for women."[17] Her book, translated and circulated internationally, marked the worldwide development of an increasingly radical consciousness among women who experienced the need for liberation.

The year 1963 also marked the opening of Vatican Council II in Rome. But the question of women's presence at the Vatican Council had not yet been raised in official circles. In her article on "The American Catholic Bishops and Woman," Antoinette Iadarola recalls how women came to infiltrate that heavily guarded male scene:

> In a truly Christian gesture, Pope John invited non-Roman Christian communicants to attend sessions of Vatican Council II as honored guests. This unprecedented gesture had an ironic twist,

---

[16] See Cardinal Roy, "Reflections on *Pacem in Terris*" in Joseph Gremillion, ed., *The Gospel of Peace and Justice: Catholic Social Teaching Since Pope John XXIII* (New York: Orbis, 1976), p. 561. The Cardinal refers to an audience of April 16, 1966, where Paul VI pointed out the originality of Pope John's approach, stating that "it is not merely a matter of a posthumous reading of the past" but of an effort "to discover, in time, signs . . . indications of a relationship with the kingdom of God. . . ."

[17] Betty Friedan, *The Feminine Mystique* (New York: W.W. Norton and Co., 1963).

for the wives of Protestant observers arrived in Rome as hostesses to bishops and some attended the debate on the floor of St. Peter's while Roman Catholic women were absent. Even the great number of women in religious communities (four times as many as men), whose customs and rules were on the Council agenda for examination, had no representation on any of the conciliar commissions. The windows were opened, but gingerly.[18]

There seems to be no record of Pope John XXIII's opinions regarding women in attendance at the council, although some ferment concerning women's place in the church was manifest shortly after the opening of Vatican II.[19] It was only at the second session of the council that the absence of women as lay auditors was noted. Perhaps it was Belgian Cardinal Leo Josef Suenens' advocacy on their behalf which resulted in an historic invitation, issued by Pope Paul VI on September 8, 1964.

> Women would be permitted to attend some sessions of the Ecumenical Council. . . . Certain nuns and leaders of Catholic women's organizations would be admitted as 'auditors' of debates of the

---

[18] Iadarola, "The American Catholic Bishops and Woman," p. 466.

[19] Mary Daly describes evidences of a change in outlook at the opening of the council in her book, *The Church and the Second Sex* (Boston: Beacon Press, 1968), pp. 123–127. She includes: the scrutiny of the press to report on signs of discrimination against women; the appearance of petitions sent to council fathers by women, including those of three German women theologians; critical articles in the liberal Catholic magazines; and new serious scholarship exposing the strong anti-feminist strain in the Christian tradition.

third session of the Council . . . on matters of interest to them.[20]

In addition to these designated auditors, an international group of feminist women organized through "St. Joan's Alliance" stood by to write up their version of the proceedings. They also submitted resolutions on the desirability of full participation of women in the church, including ordination, and a revision of canon law.[21] The noted British economist Barbara Ward was another silent observer. Although she had prepared a paper for the council fathers, she was not allowed to address them; instead, her paper was delivered at the third session by a man.[22]

Rosemary Lauer, an American scholar and professor of philosophy at St. John's University, New York, chose a public forum to pick up on the questions that were critical to women at the council. Her article on "Women and the Church" was published December 20, 1963 in *The Commonweal*.[23] In it, she reviewed interpretations of women's status in the history of the church, including the New Testament, and pursued the statement published by St. Joan's Alliance for the Vatican Council: "that priestly duties be entrusted to women as well as men; that the diaconate be restored as a permanent ministry," and "that women would be willing and eager to respond if the church extends the priesthood to them." She concludes:

---

[20] *New York Times,* September 8, 1964. Cited in Iadarola, "The American Catholic Bishops and Woman," p. 466.

[21] *Bulletin of St. Joan's Alliance,* no. 1, August 1966, New York, SSC. Cited in Iadarola, p. 475.

[22] See Albertus Magnus McGrath, *Women and the Church* (Garden City, New York: Image Books, 1976), p. 8.

[23] Rosemary Lauer, "Women and the Church," *The Commonweal* LXXIX: 13 (December 20, 1963), pp. 365–368.

> To one who thinks seriously about these things, it seems very clear that the entire question of woman's position in society and in the church needs desperately to be reconsidered in the light of the most recent findings of Scripture scholars, biologists, sociologists, anthropologists, and historians. Great strides have been made in all these areas, but it remains to synthesize the results and present a quite new picture of women and a corresponding program of action.[24]

It is hard to estimate the import of Lauer's article during this time. The only response published in *The Commonweal* came from another feminist, Mary Daly, who declared her shame that she had not written it, and shame "for all of us who should be articulate about its subject and have been silent."[25] Daly concluded with a determined commitment to pursue the issues, a commitment which has led to the strongest feminist prose in print. Lauer's article in response to proceedings at Vatican II was a clarion call for responsible analysis. Since then, questions about women's "place" and the history of their subordination in society and the church have yielded an abundance of Christian feminist literature, perhaps even beyond the dreams of Mary Daly.

## From Vatican II Until 1978

Today, more than twenty-five years after the council and the promulgation of its far-reaching documents, we can assess its impact on the consciousness and role of women by reviewing developments in the church subse-

---

[24] Lauer, p. 369.

[25] For Mary Daly's letter, see the Correspondence section of *The Commonweal*, LXXIX: 20 (February 14, 1964), p. 603. She writes: "This much I know: the beginnings of these articles and these books (how badly we need these books, especially!) are already in the minds and on the lips of many of us. And—this is both a prophecy and a promise—they will come."

quent to 1965, both in its official teaching and in the experience of women. First, it is helpful to determine what the teaching of Vatican II contributed to women's rising consciousness of their dignity and baptismal rights, and how church statements attempted to qualify that consciousness. Second, two positive results of the council which have a bearing on the topic of women's place in the church will be discussed: the ecumenical movement and the inclusion of women in Paul VI's commission on birth control. Third, the church's social teachings as they relate to women's role in the mission of the church will be explored.

## Council Documents and Church Social Teaching

The documents of Vatican II address women's situation with a curious combination of old formulations and new assurances. For example, feminist scholar Anne E. Patrick notes that in *Gaudium et Spes* there is "a decidedly androcentric bias, indeed a blindness to the (prevailing) sexism in its understanding of human rights and dignity." She also hails two key theological declarations, however, in this same document—"that God wills for society to reflect the essential equality of the sexes, and that history is the locus of the activity of God's Spirit."[26] The androcentric bias remains prevalent in American society and the church today, but the council's insistence on the full humanity of woman stands as a decided break with the old tradition which taught that she was ontologically inferior. Despite qualifying statements in the documents of Vatican II, and these are certainly numerous in the teachings of Paul VI, women took to heart the statements on their essential equality. They have voiced their desires with ever more persistence in the years following the council.

---

[26] Anne E. Patrick, SNJM. "Toward Renewing 'The Life and Culture of Fallen Man': *Gaudium et Spes* as Catalyst for Catholic Feminist Theology," in Judith Dwyer, SSJ, ed., *Questions of Special Urgency: The Church and the Modern World Two Decades after Vatican II* (Georgetown University Press, 1986), p. 57.

In Anne Patrick's judgment, "the enhanced sense of full personhood and moral and social responsibility now articulated by Catholic women, a number of whom are solidly established as professional theologians," is arguably a result of *Gaudium et Spes* even though that result may not have been anticipated by its authors.[27] Patrick cites the growing feminist critique of the tradition by loyal Catholic women. They emerged from a female population that was ripe for the affirmations of the council documents, and are making a difference today in the very theological forum which had legitimated women's subordination.[28] In addition, their scholarship, which has been made available to a wider public through conferences, workshops, study groups, and articles in mainline Catholic magazines and newspapers, has helped women in all fields to articulate more effectively their experience of oppression.

*Gaudium et Spes* and other social teachings of the church since Vatican Council II make clear that it is integral to the church's mission to confront oppressive situations and structures. Ironically, it is the growing consciousness of the systemic oppression of women in both church and society that makes the limitations in these social teachings more glaring today than previously.[29] Specifically, the language of the council documents reinforces women's invisibility through a dominant use of generic (masculine) nouns, such as *mankind* and *sons* and *brotherhood*, only occasionally addressing *men and women* in a text meant for all persons. In addition, the extensive use of male imagery for the deity both reinforces a patriarchal

---

[27] Patrick, p. 55.

[28] Patrick, p. 56. The author further notes that prior to the council the field of theology was an exclusively male preserve. Since then, she states, more than three hundred and fifty women can be numbered as "professional theologians." A review of their publications would suggest that many of these are working from a feminist perspective.

[29] Patrick. See pages 64–73.

image of the godhead and legitimizes the patriarchal structures which follow from that image. Third, through the use of such symbolic language as the Eve/Mary sign used in the traditional meaning of death and life, mother and bride (to depict the church), woman is presented in terms that do little to suggest the mutuality and equality between women and men (see, for example, *Lumen Gentium*, nn. 7, 8, 9, 56, 64). Finally, the language used in the closing messages of the council reveals that the conciliar fathers thought of and addressed women in terms of their sexual-relational roles, not in terms of their personhood or their accomplishment.

Evidence of this prevailing attitude toward women has significant implications for this study, because it helps explain the ambiguity with which the council fathers addressed the "nature" of woman. On the one hand, the council insisted on the dignity of each person and the basic equality of men and women, in virtue of their possession of a rational soul and their creation in God's image. Thus, in Patrick's analysis, the council affirmed "a more dynamic, historically conscious understanding of God's will than had previously held sway in post-Reformation Catholicism, with all that this implies in terms of openness to the genuinely *new*."[30] Conciliar teachings proclaim that while God makes the future possible, men and women are co-responsible for that future. The teachings emphasize that the main traits of the human person which must be respected in order to contribute to the dignity of each man and woman are: the dignity of the mind, the dignity of the moral conscience, and authentic freedom.[31]

---

[30] Patrick, p. 58.

[31] See especially Chapter 1 of *Gaudium et Spes*, nn. 12–22. For a good discussion of the contradictory structural realities of the church in relation to these principles, see Katherine Meagher, SC, "Women in Relation to Orders and Jurisdiction," in James Coriden, ed., *Sexism and Church Law* (New York: Paulist Press, 1977), pp. 31–41.

On the other hand, the rights of woman are specified as those compatible with her "special nature," understood through a unique set of personal traits evident in her behavior. Not surprisingly, these relate mainly to her role as nurturer in the family. This role as understood by the council (and, as we will see, similarly interpreted by some U.S. bishops in their pastoral letters) is well summarized by Nadine Foley:

> It is a role of complementarity with men whose educative influence in the family is necessary but secondary. The familial role of women is essential and normative. All other possibilities which may open to women through sociocultural development are legitimate for her to the extent that her complement of unique 'feminine' qualities can be expressed in a nurturing supportive capacity.[32]

Perceiving women's role to be one of complementarity, the hierarchy takes on the special responsibility of championing their rights, in order to preserve their dignity in that role. Hence, the official church teaching on woman is based on a doctrine that biological differences established in the divine order of creation must be definitive of women and their social roles. It follows that the fixed, inescapable role for woman is to be subordinate to man. In such teaching about women, the church gives primacy to its notion of divine revelation, rather than to the believing persons in the community.

This is where the women's movement may be said to be on a collision course with the institutional church, because the basic tenets of the movement are founded on a different view. Woman is seen to be, above all else, a person with a basic right to self-determination, and what can be

---

[32] Nadine Foley, OP, "Women in Vatican Documents," in James Coriden, ed., *Sexism and Church Law*, p. 98.

said of one woman cannot be attributed to all women. Rather, each individual manifests a unique complement of human characteristics, running the gamut of expression from "feminine" to "masculine." When the church singles out *woman* as a distinct category among human persons, and describes *her* in universal terms without regard to individual personality traits, inappropriate sex role differentiations are made that are not grounded in contemporary experience. Woman's role is so defined by the church in order to protect an ideal of the family. This definition effectively excludes her, however, from the ordained sacramental ministry and subsequent participation in policy-making and decision-making.

## *Ecumenism and the Question of Women's Participation*

In contrast to the above mentioned problematic areas within the council documents and social teaching, two results of Vatican II must be highlighted here. They have had continuing influence down to our time and an important bearing on the role of women in society and in the church. The first is the growing ecumenical spirit, stemming from Pope John XXIII's largesse in inviting non-Roman Christian communicants to attend the council. The second is the openly-discussed question of women's inclusion in policy-making bodies in the church, followed by their unprecedented contribution to the papal commission on birth control.

Since the council, a growing ecumenical consciousness has developed through dialogue on every level. One example is the Christian feminist movement, which is strongly ecumenical and claims Protestant as well as Catholic scholars working out a distinctive theology of liberation from a feminist perspective. Collaboration has strengthened both the scholarship and the momentum for liberation. Theologian Anne Carr observes the similar approaches of these scholars:

They use the central and liberating Gospel message of equality, mutuality, and service and their own experience to criticize those elements in the tradition which capitulate to take-for-granted patriarchal norms. And they use the central biblical tradition of justice and equality to criticize sexist patterns and practices in culture and society.[33]

In addition to widespread ecumenical exchange among women and other scholars in feminist scholarship, there has been significant dialogue among church officials concerning the ecumenical ramifications of women's ordination to the priesthood. With the ordination of women in the Anglican Church in 1974, compelling theological discourse has heightened the consciousness of male leaders within that denomination and has forced a debate with the Roman Catholic hierarchy who seek reconciliation with the Anglican Church. A series of four letters (July 9, 1975 to March 23, 1976) between Anglican Archbishop Donald Coggan of Canterbury and Pope Paul VI offers key insights into the ecumenical ramifications of women's ordination.[34] Ten years later, a highly nuanced exchange is recorded between Cardinal Willebrands and Archbishop Robert Runcie.[35] Generally, dialogue occurred around the central question whether issues related to the eucharist and the ordained ministry are doctrinal or disciplinary. Paul VI's reassertion of traditional strictures against women's ordination[36] did not end the debate; conferences continue to be

---

[33] Anne Carr, BVM, "Coming of Age in Christianity: Women and the Churches," in *The Furrow* 34 (June 1983), pp. 347–351.

[34] *Origins*, Vol. 6: No. 9 (August 12, 1976).

[35] *Origins*, Vol. 16: No. 8 (July 17, 1986).

[36] *Origins*, Vol. 6: No. 33 (February 3, 1977). The pope declared that a "natural resemblance" must be maintained between Christ and his priest, and stated: ". . . if the role of Christ were not taken by a man . . . it would be difficult to see in the minister the image of Christ. For Christ himself was and remains a man."

held on this question[37] and will likely continue. The 1977 Vatican declaration undermined many people's confidence in Vatican guidance on women's issues; they remain skeptical even when it is put forth with the rhetorical power and persistence of Pope John Paul II. The Vatican position met its fullest challenge to date with the consecration of Rev. Barbara Harris as an Episcopal bishop on February 11, 1989, in Boston—an event which broke a barrier for all the major branches of Christianity.

The last point that must be made in relation to Vatican Council II is the effect of women's presence/non-presence there and their subsequent historic influence on church discourse about the morality of birth control.

First of all, while women were only silent observers at the council in whatever capacity they attended (whether as wives of non-Catholic clergymen, as journalists, or later as specially invited auditors), their very presence spoke. In part this was owing to the careful scrutiny of the press, which picked up on such incidents as the barring of women from attending the council mass during the first session, and of a woman journalist from receiving communion at a council mass during the second session. Such episodes revealed Vatican officials' offensive and antiquated view of woman. When reported, the incidents and the attitudes they represented received widespread criticism.[38]

Secondly, the third session of the council saw the development of the Pastoral Constitution on the Church,

---

[37] See the article, "Conference asks if church opposes women's ordination," in the *National Catholic Reporter*, May 1, 1987, p. 4. The ecumenical conference was held at Heythrop College, University of London. In the exchange between two male Anglicans and three Roman Catholics (two of them women), several authoritative points were made, among them: that *diakonein,* the Greek verb meaning *to minister,* is used in the New Testament of Jesus (he came to minister, not to be ministered unto), of angels (after the temptations in the desert), and of women. It is not used of the apostles.

[38] Daly, *The Church and the Second Sex*, p. 123.

*Gaudium et Spes*, and heard a number of visionary statements concerning women. Only one American prelate, Archbishop Hallinan of Atlanta, offered an opinion on the question of women in the church. He developed a full proposal which recommended women lectors and acolytes, women in the role of deacon, women as teachers and consultants in theology, and women as participants within organizations created to implement Vatican II teachings. In particular, the archbishop pointed out that the community between man and woman must not be one of subservience, but one of harmony, mutual respect, love, and responsibility.[39] Unfortunately, Archbishop Hallinan's proposal never reached the floor, although it was filed with the council's general secretariat and given wide press coverage.[40]

Perhaps it was Hallinan's insistence on the inclusion of women in future commissions that eventually led to the contribution of women in the papal commission on birth control. The silence of women in Vatican gatherings was broken. In the documented story of the commission, which covers a twenty-year period of church debate and ruling on contraception, Kaiser reports his own reading of postulata (wishes for change, or requests) that were written to the council fathers. He found in them no indication that "a single Catholic bishop ever handed on a request that the church relax its strictures against contraception."[41] But no more than four years later, the papal commission urged Paul VI to change the church's traditional teaching on birth control.[42] What happened to influence the minds of churchmen who evidently had felt that the church's teaching could not change on this issue?

---

[39] *The Catholic Citizen*, Vol. LI, no. 10, November–December 1965, p. 88. Cited in full in George Tavard, *Woman in Christian Tradition* (Notre Dame: University of Notre Dame Press, 1973), pp. 127–128.

[40] Daly, *The Church and the Second Sex*, p. 131.

[41] Kaiser, p. 5.

[42] Kaiser, p. 141.

## A Century of Struggle for Women

Kaiser's documentation of the process indicates that the testimony of women and their spontaneous interventions during the commission's proceedings were essential to this shift. The women spoke of a couple's "natural rhythm" for lovemaking, of the marvelous moments of communion and their effect on family equilibrium, of the unworkability of the rhythm method of contraception, and of woman's inability to predict her next period during menopause. They urged the theologians and bishops present to consider what "free and responsible Christians" felt about children: "Couples want children and will have them generously and love them. They do not need the impetus of legislation to procreate. It is the very instinct of life, love and sexuality."[43] Collette Potvin encouraged the commission to see sex as a part of God's commandment to love one another:

> Where I come from, we marry primarily to live with a man of our choice. Children are a normal consequence of our love and not the goal. The physiological integrity of the conjugal act is less important than the repercussions of that love on the couple and on their family. And that conjugal act is the principal way we have of showing our love for each other.[44]

Kaiser's report demonstrates the quality of women's reflection on their experience which many of these churchmen listened to for the first time. They heard so well, in fact, that such noted theologians as Josef Fuchs and Bernard Häring, who acknowledged that the papal commission study had influenced the change in their position on the morality of contraception, led the majority vote in favor of a change in church teaching on the issue. They were joined by such distinguished members of the hierar-

---

[43] Cited in Kaiser, p. 141.
[44] Cited in Kaiser, p. 141.

chy as Cardinal Suenens, and Cardinal Shehan of Baltimore, who said, "The church grows, the church develops. And the *sensus fidelium* plays a big role in that development. The church must recognize how marriage is lived out today."[45]

Despite the conclusion of the papal commission study, which reflected the changes, a seven-member minority opinion held sway with the pope. He was persuaded by their arguments to reaffirm the Catholic Church's traditional teaching on birth control, which prohibits the use of any method of fertility control other than the rhythm method. Also, perhaps, willing to abort the reasoned process in order to maintain the authority of Peter, Paul VI issued the encyclical *Humanae Vitae,* which for many was seen to falsify human experience.[46]

A review of the commission's proceedings makes a good case study of the official church's fear of change and its isolation from "the world" which the council addressed with such compassion. It also supports the conclusion that bishops and churchmen changed their minds when they listened to women whose experience and insights inserted a whole new dimension into moral discourse. Once presumed to be silent, acquiescent, and supportive of ecclesiastical authority, women trusted their experience and spoke up in opposition to "official" Catholic teachings on conception control. Women, it is clear, bring a requisite reality testing to such areas of study as the meaning of sexuality.

## *Social Teachings After the Council*

The decade following Vatican Council II abounded with social teachings in the form of encyclicals and pastorals

---

[45] Cited in Kaiser, p. 164.

[46] Kaiser reports that couples, priests, even bishops, were to leave the church in the wake of this decision. British theologian Charles Davis, "who saw very clearly how radically the official church was opting for authority at the expense of truth," was among those to leave (p. 164).

and addresses which sought to read the complex of facts relevant to human rights and personal freedom, and, more particularly, women's role in society and in the church. It is beyond the scope of this book to analyze these statements in full, but a brief survey will provide additional pertinent background for the U.S. bishops' pastorals written between 1974 and 1987. Statements before 1971, for example, speak of human rights in a markedly generic fashion and also address the changes in women's role in institutions outside the church. Later statements address women's participation more specifically, sometimes delineating at length those qualities which are named as "feminine" and God-given. The question occurs: Why does the official church persist in qualifying for woman that which can be said generically of the human person?

For example, in *Pacem et Terris* (1963), Pope John XXIII states what is intrinsic to human personhood and offers an enumeration of the fundamental rights of human persons (nn. 9–27). In *Populorum Progressio,* Pope Paul VI states what must be guaranteed to individual persons and infers that it is God's design for each person to come to maturity, to become fully a person, through the use of intelligence and freedom (n. 15). *Humanae Vitae* recognizes new cultural trends: "a change is also seen both in the manner of considering the person of woman and her place in society" (n. 20). Only in the synodal document *The Ministerial Priesthood and Justice in the World* (1971) is there a specific concern expressed for women's participation in the household of the church.

The decade of the 1970s saw a remarkable increase in the church's preoccupation with woman and her role. Pope Paul VI made at least a dozen significant statements about woman, some of them fully developed. These included the address to the convention of the Union of Italian Catholic Jurists on "The Role of Women in Contemporary Society" in 1974; a document in 1975 on "The Role of Women in Church and Society; Disciples and Co-Workers"; and a statement in 1976 on "Women/Balancing Rights and

Duties."[47] In 1976 the Vatican issued three additional statements on women in the church: a statement on "The Role of Women" by the Papal Commission of the Vatican Congregation for the Evangelization of Peoples; a Papal Biblical Commission Report entitled "Can Women Be Priests?"; and the report from the Doctrine on the Faith known as the "Declaration on the Question of the Admission of Women to the Ministerial Priesthood."[48]

A survey of this literature indicates that while important new developments in human consciousness are seeking appropriate inclusion in the continuing experience of the church, they are considered matter for comment and interpretation by a teaching church. In the above mentioned documents, the operative principles which are applied are those of woman's specific feminine nature, her unique qualities as a woman, and her appropriate service in auxiliary roles.[49] Because the official texts appear to be incompatible with women's realizations as they subject their experience to critical examination in the light of the gospel, it is predictable that tension will heighten between those who articulate the new vision and others who apply the traditional teaching. The question is: How will the new paradigm break through the logjam of existing thoughts and beliefs, insistently held together by an unyielding leadership?

Some think that if those who articulate the new vision are persistent enough, they will succeed in bringing about change. They found hope in the decade of the 1970s when the Vatican position developed to the degree that women

---

[47] See *The Pope Speaks*, XIX (December 8, 1974); *Origins*, Vol. 4: No. 45 (May 1, 1975), p. 718; and *Origins*, Vol. 5: No. 35 (February 19, 1976), p. 552.

[48] See *Origins*, Vol. 5: No. 44 (April 22, 1976), 703–704; *Origins*, Vol. 6: No. 6 (July 1, 1976), pp. 92–96; and *Origins*, Vol. 6: No. 33 (February 3, 1977), p. 524.

[49] Foley, "Women in Vatican Documents," pp. 93–94.

could be given a form of pastoral jurisdiction and also allowed to exercise leadership in various forms of liturgical worship. Women came to be seen as capable of exercising a ministry of word and sacrament. Moreover, circumstances forced the sharing of women and married men in regular pastoral tasks, while dwindling numbers of priests have forced ordained ministers to concentrate more on the particular ministry of the sacraments.

Another view is that major change occurs with a leap to a new level of perception. A paradigm shift occurs. Then the thought process is realigned and a new and more inclusive framework of perceiving results. How open are the U.S. bishops to such a change? They are writing from the American experience and culture as well as in the light of Vatican statements, and they seek to address the issues which are important to women. Between the years 1974 and 1987 when the twelve pastoral letters were written, a wide variety of meetings, with varying agenda, highlighted women's issues for both hierarchy and laity. Three World Conferences of Women were held, in Mexico (1975), Copenhagen (1980), and Nairobi (1985). In the U.S., two sessions of the Women's Ordination Conference occurred (1975 and 1979); Congress voted against the ERA (1982) and saw its reintroduction; the official body of Catholic bishops (NCCB) voted unanimously to write a pastoral on women in church and society (1983); two sessions of the National Conference on Women in the Church (1986 and 1987) were held in Washington, D.C.; and a multi-cultural Womanchurch Speaks Conference met twice, in Chicago (1983) and Cincinnati (1987). In addition, a Women's Theological Center was established. These events spawned an ever more clearly articulated vision of what women seek. Feminist Maria Riley sums it up well:

> It is not merely that women want equal rights and equal opportunity. What we really want is that our experiences as women enter equally and mutually into the human endeavor, both in the Church and

in the world. We are also aware, in the core of our being, of what our absence at the centers of power and decision-making have meant; the human family sees with one eye, hears with one ear, walks on one leg, and works with one hand.[50]

Writing within this immediate context, the U.S. bishops face a particular challenge. The question of women's full participation in the church requires a reading of the complex of facts in our present social situation. Will the bishops try to open up still further the teaching of Vatican II? For example, in their local churches, are they able to guide discipleship based on baptismal commitment and personal gifts viewed in conjunction with the needs of the community? Will they bless the creative internal development in the church at the grass roots level that has begun the work of transformation?

The next chapter offers an interpretation of some U.S. bishops' basic views toward the role of women today, as these are disclosed in metaphorical statements in their pastoral letters. The discussion is offered not to categorize and label, since it is by no means comprehensive or exhaustive. It is an effort to provide useful handles and deeper insights. A later chapter analyzes the findings of the study with reference to the historical survey in this chapter, in an effort to discover the extent to which these U.S. bishops call us in the U.S. church to a new vision of ministry and community.

---

[50] Maria Riley, OP, *Women: Carriers of a New Vision* (Washington, DC: Center of Concern, n.d.), p. 4.

## Chapter 2

# Metaphors in the Pastorals

In the previous chapter, we saw that the question of women's role in the church has acquired particular importance in recent times. Since the mid-1970s, women's participation in the church's mission, as expressed through an increasing variety of ministries, has been a focus of study and reflection all over the world, but nowhere, perhaps, as intensely as in the United States. This is due to the struggles for equality in society and in the church that U.S. women have waged in this century, and the Vatican Council's affirmation of women's essential equality with men as human persons. It is also due to the wealth of feminist theological scholarship aimed at recovering the liberating strains within Christian tradition.

Nevertheless, while enjoying widespread recognition and an ever increasing acceptance in their new roles, women find in many circles the familiar, stubborn defense of patriarchy which yet holds sway in the church and in society. Does the view of the present U.S. hierarchy toward women in the church differ substantially from the views explored in the last chapter? The purpose here is to study the metaphors in twelve recent pastoral letters to determine what difference there might be.

That we are witnessing the disintegration of western civilization and at the same time the emergence of a new understanding of humanity, particularly the feminine dimension, is attested to by many thinkers today. Some cultural historians, scientists, and psychologists have expressed this evolution/revolution within their own disciplines.[1] The

---

[1] See, for example, the writings of the physicist Fritjof Capra, *The Turning Point: Science, Society, and the Rising Culture* (New York: Bantam, 1983); of social analyst Joe Holland, "The Spiritual Crisis of Modern Culture" (Washington, D.C., Center of Concern, 1983); and of Jungian psychologist, Marion Woodman,

church itself, which has grown and developed in the context of western civilization, also shows signs of decline. One sign is the loss of flexibility, an inability to adapt to changing situations. How, then, can church leaders take a fresh approach to present day structures in order to accommodate the fuller self-knowledge of its people?

In the light of the changes occurring at all levels of society and within the church, and despite the impasse that women experience in attempting to dialogue with Vatican officials, some U.S. bishops have braved a study of the role of women in the church today. We are clearly at a crossroads, where old certainties are questioned radically and new ideas are being forged with a mixture of caution and courage. Given the intrinsic limitations of being male when writing about women, what can the bishops say that will shed light on our situation? Have they recognized that something new is being born and must have its own place in time?

With a close study of the content and form of the twelve pastorals, the reader becomes mindful of the particular vocabulary and images used. The language that the bishops give to their experience is particularly engaging. Language, ever the architect of social forms, discloses its own meaning. Through metaphor, for example, language can create, evoke, or maintain an ideology or paradigm. Some metaphors in the pastorals evoke powerful images and reveal the bishops' prevailing ideologies of women. While a number of these reinforce the church's traditional view of women, some help us entertain new possibilities for women's gifts for ministry and for relationship. It is proposed here that a study of metaphors provides a valuable hermeneutic for discovering the relationship between the historical situation and the statements made about it, and the relationship of present-day questions with current history.

---

*The Pregnant Virgin* (Toronto: Inner City Books, 1985). Each author affirms that the cultural recovery of the feminine, along with the consequent transformation of male and female roles, is what may save us from self-annihilation.

Metaphor as a linguistic device contains the power to further understanding and to open up a new way of looking at reality. In particular, a metaphor images reality as it is perceived in the most ordinary way, by transposing meaning from one context to another. The images created either shatter previous understandings or shape brand new ones.[2] In the process, a metaphor seems to draw the imagination into a particular logic.[3] Modern language philosophers and philologists seem to agree that metaphors are indeed carriers of the assumptions individuals use to interpret their experiences.[4] These writers distinguish three

---

[2] See Bernard J.F. Lonergan, *Insight: A Study of Human Understanding* (San Francisco: Harper and Row, 1958), pp. 8–9, 10, 16, 18, 34–35. The image, drawn from the level of human sense experience, provides the data that, through the questioning spirit, give rise to the insight. This is the pivotal moment of the dynamic movement toward understanding. Focusing on metaphor is a way of acknowledging the centrality of image in insight. The image as symbol constitutes a heuristic technique. It anticipates what is unfolding toward a new understanding.

[3] For a thorough discussion of metaphor as a vehicle in discourse see Paul Ricoeur, *The Rule of Metaphor*, trans. Robert Czerny (Toronto: University of Toronto, 1975). For a playful discussion of the role of metaphor in contemporary discourse and quotable quotes on metaphor, see Nelle Morton, *The Journey Is Home* (Boston: Beacon Press, 1985), pp. 152–170, 210–227.

[4] See especially Michael Mochs and W. Calvin Fields, "Developing a Content Analysis for Interpreting Language Use in Organizations," in *Research in the Sociology of Organizations* (Greenwich, CT: JAI Press, Inc., 1985, vol. 4), pp. 81–126. The authors developed a research method designed to identify particular subjects' implicit theories-in-use, believing that the method will allow researchers to make informed inferences concerning the theories held. The theorists contend that metaphors may be important carriers of schemata, or sets of unexamined assumptions individuals use to interpret their experiences. See pp. 83–84. They demonstrate how linguistic devices enact and maintain the nature of organized life. I am grateful to Jean Bartunek for suggesting the usefulness of this article.

types of metaphors which generate meanings: (1) orientation metaphors (e.g. those that define perceptual fields), (2) ontological metaphors (e.g. those that attribute characteristics or relationships to elements), and (3) devices which involve a transfer of meaning from person or personalities to physical objects, such as metonymy and personification.

Some examples from the pastoral letters may be cited to distinguish these types. Bishop Dozier, the prime metaphorist among the bishops who wrote pastorals on women in the church, wrote that as a local bishop he "*felt crowded by the urgency of the many needs* of the Christian community."[5] As a linguistic analogy, the metaphoric phrase, "felt crowded by the urgency of the many needs," gives us a picture of the bishop, pushed against on all sides, looking for space apart from the community's needs—which are only identified as having an urgency which presses on him. By attributing "urgency" and the power to "crowd" to the abstract noun "needs," Dozier speaks metaphorically and generates an image which gives the sense of what he is feeling. This is an example of an ontological metaphor.

A second type of metaphor which generates meanings is the orientation metaphor. It defines perceptual fields, such as in Archbishop Borders' image of "our capacity *to rise above* the limitations of human life" (1), in which the possibility of transcendence has a spatial quality. Because the extra-terrestrial is imaged as skyward, humans think of "rising above" earth-bound experiences in a metaphor which images an upward physical extension.

---

[5] Most Reverend Carroll T. Dozier, *Woman: Intrepid and Loving* (Memphis, Tennessee, Epiphany 1975), p. 5. Henceforth, I will insert in parenthesis in the text the page number of the pastoral letter from which the quotation is drawn. The only exception to this procedure will be in the case of Bishop Clark, whose pastoral letter has numbered paragraphs to which I will refer. For the author, title, place and date of publication of each pastoral, the reader is referred to Exhibit A. For the identification of the metaphor in the quotation, the reader is referred to the corresponding Table; metaphors are italicized.

A third type of metaphor includes personification and metonymy, devices which involve a transfer of meaning from person or personalities to physical objects. An example may be observed in Archbishop Weakland's pastoral. He invites "all of you faithful to see this report as *getting to the heart* of one of the most important challenges facing the Church in our day—one upon which the Church's credibility in the future will depend." The archbishop sees the task force report as "getting to the heart" of an important challenge. This is a metaphor we use readily. "To get to the heart" of something means to touch its life-pulse, in a manner similar to touching the heart of a human person or animal. And the task force report does touch the issues that are critical to the life of the church today. Bishop Clark's description of the lives of "the anonymous but dauntless women of the gospel" as "*alabaster jars of nard poured out in active service . . .*" (94) is an example of metonymy, a metaphorical device which uses one entity to refer to another.

In observing how metaphors work, I noted that generally they have an appealing flavor of originality. While much of what is said in the pastoral letters is familiar, a restatement of the Catholic faith as it has been taught and lived for centuries, when something new or exceptional is introduced it is often through metaphor. Conversely, some metaphors reinforce the unspoken notions that hold our culture in a viselike grip. Finally, the use of metaphor sometimes obscures the image of reality. Then it serves to distance the speaker from the listener, because it is difficult to decipher and the meaning cannot be reached.

If it is through metaphor that implicit theories are asserted, then a study of the metaphors used in the pastorals could lead to a discovery of the bishops' unique contribution to the discussion of women's role at this time in history. Reading their metaphors is like trying to read the subtext, trying to discover the basis of their collective epistemology. It may be that their base is adequate to create a renewed vision of church that includes women at every level. It may be that a study of the basic ideology will point to the necessity of developing a new Christian anthropology, a new understanding of human sexuality, and a reformed ecclesiology.

It must be noted that the bishops' theories arise from their experience as male authorities in a church which has a two thousand year history of relegating women to subordinate roles. In addition, their approach to their topic was influenced by their experience of women and the climate of opinion about women's roles today, in their local churches. The question must be raised as to whether these bishops speak out now because they cannot remain silent in the face of the oppression women experience. Do they write because they want to participate in the emancipatory project?

## *Compiling and Classifying the Metaphors*

The method employed in studying the use of metaphor in the episcopal letters was fairly straightforward. First, all the metaphors in the twelve pastoral letters were compiled. Then, four main topics emerged under which the images could be readily grouped and studied. They are: Women and Culture; Women and the Church; Women and Men; and Conversion and Reconciliation. These topics constitute the major differentiations of the question under study. Each of them offers a different perspective on woman's being in the world and in the church. An operative assumption in this discussion is that by giving a central role to the bishops' metaphors, we can identify characteristic ways in which churchmen have thought about women during an important period of renewal. Later, the question will be raised about the degree of openness to change which church officials express in regard to women's place in the church.

Among the numerous metaphors (see Tables 1, 2, 3, 4, corresponding to the topics named above) the dominant and representative metaphors were selected for discussion in this chapter. They are classified in sub-categories so as to further specify their content. In Tables 1 and 2, these sub-categories correspond to the *past,* the *present,* and the *future,* so that patterns of these images and the shape of reality they reveal in a particular time frame can be explored.

# I. Women and Culture

In this paper, *culture* is understood to mean that web of common meanings and values which informs the consciousness/unconsciousness of a people, and which is embodied in structures in the form of myth or symbol or affect. As such, culture may be viewed as an intersection of theology and sociology, an important arena of interest to many writers today, including Pope John Paul II, whose addresses and encyclicals frequently illuminate his appreciation of the influence of culture in the life of the local church. Several assumptions are operative in the discussion of "Women and Culture." The first is that both women and men are not only shaped by today's culture but are also shapers of that culture. Secondly, men have been the predominant actors in influencing culture. A third assumption is that most people recognize in culture various social barriers which still hold women back from exploring their full capacities. Among the variety of metaphors in this study which depict the relationship between women and culture, there are some which disclose women's subordination in history. Others depict present day realities, and several have a future orientation. The metaphors will be discussed in these three sub-categories to see how they are related, and what can be learned from them.

## *Women and Culture: Historical Perspectives*

Of woman herself, it is recognized that any "idealized" image of her "denies woman her sovereign dignity" (Maher: 6) and that when she was philosophically endowed with elevated ideals, virtues and wisdom as in Proverbs 8:22, "woman was reduced on the practical level—to the situation of a legal and social minor, discriminated against as a basic threat to man." (Maher: 7) In the first metaphor, the personified "idealized image" is recognized as having power at once to elevate woman and to deny her the full human dignity which is rightfully hers. The metaphor captures the ironic effect of an idealized image as well as its power to negate the true and inherent worth of half the human species. In the second metaphor, the ironic effect is noted more specifically. "Woman" is said to have been "reduced on the practical level," that is, relegated to the status of minors who have no rights. The metaphor then leads us to image "woman," at once elevated and reduced, as a threat to man, who was responsible for the idealized image.

These two metaphors depict two ways in which society has refused to accept women. While women have been exalted beyond possibility of recognition, their status and role in concrete form lose reality and specificity. Thus, women are prevented from discovering and realizing their authentic call and historic potential when feminine characteristics are absolutized.[6]

Other metaphors which offer an historical perspective on society's treatment of women include the analogy that "prejudice is passed from generation to generation, becoming enshrined in time as tradition and social custom, seldom questioned and challenged." (Maher: 9) The personification of "prejudice" (an attitude) as being handed on as a precious legacy to one's descendants interprets an experience common to all peoples, and the irony of "enshrining" such a negative attitude is underlined. Maher implies that this legacy takes on the status of the

---

[6] See Leonardo Boff, O.F.M., *The Maternal Face of God: The Feminine and Its Religious Expressions* (San Francisco: Harper and Row, 1987), p. 33. Boff speaks of these two ways of refusing to accept woman and shows how they are "a veiled form of discrimination and domination—even in the realm of the mariological. Theologians who, however unconsciously, toil in the service of male power interests, represent Mary only as the woman who knew how to say yes—'Fiat mihi . . .'—the woman who resigned herself to fulfilling the will of God, the woman who, in modesty and anonymity, remained hidden among her household chores."

## Metaphors in the Pastorals

holy which is neither questioned nor challenged. Similarly, Borders states that men and women of every age are "not only conditioned by a culture; to a certain extent they are prisoners of a culture." (5) By using a term which conjures up graphic images of prison bars, a locked door, and a keeper, to explain culture's grip on human beings throughout history, Borders suggests that cultural conditions as we know them (i.e. men's domination of women) will never change—that men's and women's free will and self-determination cannot escape the forces of culture. A third metaphor reveals a similar view. The Minnesota bishops assert their belief that "society's pattern for women is pre-set." (8) "Pre-set" suggests a mechanical timer, such as that on electrical equipment, which requires no further consideration or decisions. The three metaphors above are alike in their representation of cultural conditions as inexorably in place.

In marked contrast to the above picture, a strong gospel note is sounded in three other metaphors found in the pastorals. Dozier states that "Jesus never once bowed to the cultural prejudices of his time that would have prohibited him from dealing with the woman of Samaria, Mary of Magdala. . . ." (4) Buswell asserts that "Jesus' teachings as they related to women contradicted some of the most time-honored practices and prejudices of the Jews." (2) Balke and Lucker refer to the status of women in Palestine at the time of Christ and state that a description of their situation would "emphasize how counter Jesus went to the culture of his time" in his attitudes toward women. (4) In these metaphors we have a picture of the historical Christ as he encountered cultural barriers which could have kept women distant from him and he from them; he "refused to bow" (pay homage) to cultural biases; his teachings spoke against practices endorsed through time; he went "counter" (opposing or striking back) to the culture of his time. Through these metaphors, Dozier, Buswell, Balke and Lucker emphasize the decidedly counter-cultural nature of Jesus' own ministry with women, his relationship with them as well as his teachings about them.

In several pastorals there are metaphors which seek to render women's own experiences in society. Maher, for example, personifies the media to illustrate how women contribute to their own exploitation "by their response to . . . the suggestiveness, immature appeal and insidious pressures of the communications and entertainment media in their presentation of 'feminine' models of behavior, thought and dress." (10) Here the media are imbued with the power to pressure, lure, and arouse women. This power is not neutral: it is seen as "immature" and "insidious" and as presenting models which some might view as feminine but which this author decries, as evidenced in the quotation marks around the word. With this metaphor, Maher seems to imply that women, by adopting the image of woman carried in the media, take on a false image created for the consumer, and that women are responsible for having adopted that image.

An extended metaphor which delineates women's experience in society is found in Weakland's task force report. In a summary account of their conversations with women, members of the task force try to give voice to women's own experience:

> Women were not encouraged to bond with other women, for one binds oneself not to weakness but to strength. Women have been socialized to base their security in the self-assurance and good judgment of men . . . in many cases women derived their self-esteem from the approval they received from men . . . this situation has fostered a spirit of competition among women so that they vie with one another for men's attention, not so much to win men as to find for themselves some sense of esteem and security. (3A)

The notion of "bonding" as it is emphasized in women's groups today recognizes that women have been separated from one another in partriarchal systems and have not enjoyed the solidarity that men experience. In the metaphorical phrase "one binds oneself not to weakness but to strength . . ." the image evoked is that of individual women, identifying in themselves either physical or moral or psychological weakness, who fasten themselves to men who are perceived as strong in the areas in which they themselves are weak. Next, there is an image of women standing secure in the approval and good judgment of men. A third image is that of women trying to win out over one another for the attention of those men on whom their sense of esteem and security is perceived to depend.

In the above selection of metaphorical statements which represent an historical perspective on women and culture, several patterns are evident. Through metaphors, the bishops show how woman's idealized image at once elevates her status and reduces her role in ordinary life. They illustrate the fact that both men and women are victims of prejudice, which is viewed, on the one hand, as immutably fixed in culture and, on the other hand, as deliberately overcome by Jesus. In metaphorical images, women are depicted as contributing to their own exploitation by adopting the image of woman presented by the media and by seeking their security outside themselves. In sum, these images disclose the male monopoly on cultural definition, a monopoly which renders woman the silent object of that defining, passively dependent upon men who prescribe her role. They also reveal the historical breakthrough of Jesus' recognition and treatment of women as persons.

## *Women and Culture: Present Day Perspectives*

Some of the dominant metaphors related to the topic of "Women and Culture" may be identified as "orientation metaphors," that is, devices which orient individuals in space and time. These metaphors constitute a set of unquestioned assumptions about the nature of reality, casting the experiences of current events in terms made familiar through the experience of the past. In this study, such metaphors give us a picture of women's new consciousness as it relates to culture today.

Maher offers several orientation metaphors. These situate the reader in the particular character of this time in history. He writes of the "demand of this technological age for women to assume new and different positions and responsibilities" (3) and states his view that "women's developing awareness of the unique personhood of human beings is provoking them to dissatisfaction with previously tolerated or accepted female roles and images." (4) In the first metaphor, Maher says it is "this technological age" which demands a change in women's role; thus we are led to understand the pressures of our time, specifically related to developments in science, in regard to cultural changes in women's occupations and role. In the second metaphor, Maher offers a further insight, asserting that "women's developing awareness . . . is provoking them to dissatisfaction. . . ." This statement suggests that the cause of women's dissatisfaction is to be found in their raised consciousness. These two metaphors invite us to consider philosophically "this technological age" and "women's developing awareness" as the primary agents in bringing about change today.

Further orientation metaphors may be found in Dozier's letter. He situates his readers in a universal context when he writes of "the forces that place women upon the world stage and make 'women' a live issue today in the international consciousness." (1) Further on he proclaims that "Woman's awakening is indeed as global as inflation." (3) In the first statement, women are twice viewed as objects, not agents. First, they are affected by some unnamed energy ("forces") which makes them actors, and then they are objectified as a *live issue* (as in *live wire*— something one does not want to touch). In the second statement, the metaphorical analogy of woman's awakening with global inflation contains an element of surprise. While the word *inflation* renders a negative interpretation (a situation which does no one any good and which must be quelled, not encouraged), when joined with *global* it succeeds in presenting an image of the widespread effect of women's new consciousness, which shakes the foundations of our most basic systems and leaves no one unaffected. Women are no longer asleep. Their awakened consciousness is here to stay and demands adjustments on every level of society.

Two additional metaphors from Dozier's pastoral offer images that the mind can readily perceive. He writes that "Rejection and frustration heightened the demand for rightful equality." (1) Here, the terms *rejection* and *frustration* refer to emotions experienced as entities without a physical referent, the sources of an increasing demand for equality. The term *equality* as modified by *rightful* further increases the justifiability of the demand. Further on, Dozier states that "For the woman, the narrow institutions of the past seem more dispensable than ever, because woman has discovered her sister. Their mutual embrace reaches around the world; it is feminist, reverential, even ecclesial." (3) In the first sentence, the impersonal noun *institutions* is given the connotation of being narrow and dispensable. The reason, Dozier explains, is women's newly-discovered sisterhood which he then characterizes in terms of a worldwide mutual embrace. The embrace is personified in a final metaphoric action that surprises; it is given a trilogy of attributes: feminist, reverential, and even (he gives the impression of having hesitated before using the word, and then emphasizes it) ecclesial. Dozier the metaphorist seeks to establish that women's bonding is new, with a quality of the proverbial "eureka!" which is then transmitted through hugs or a hand-grasp by women in every nation. The embrace itself carries a further interpretation with the three qualities attributed to it, each of them abstract in itself but carrying substantive meaning when attributed to women's worldwide embrace. The word *feminist* refers to an attitude or worldview which seeks to promote women's equality with men. *Reverential* connotes deep respect and picks up on the word *Reverend*, a clerical title. *Ecclesial* pertains to the church and also to the clergy. By juxtaposing these three attributes, Dozier suggests their compatibility.

Additional orientation metaphors are found in the letter of the Minnesota bishops. In one statement they assert that "neither society nor church can any longer tolerate the imposition of barriers in women's paths of growth." (6) In another statement, the bishops affirm that "ours is a culture which rightly stresses personhood, and persons cannot be so stereotyped, especially on the basis of sex, that they fit neatly into pre-ordained roles." (15) The first of these statements personifies society and the church as subjects of the verbal phrase "can any longer tolerate" and couples them with the imagistic phrases, "imposition of barriers" and "women's paths of growth." The metaphoric image in these statements depicts a view of society and the church as taking responsibility to remove the visible obstacles to women's development. Culture is thus personified as recognizing the individual as a person who cannot be made to fit a role for which he or she is unsuited.

Lastly, there are metaphors in Clark's pastoral which impart further information about the cultural causes of our new consciousness. In the image, "rape and violence against women are on the rise," there is a sense that rape and violence are entities growing larger and more threatening to women specifically, and Clark states that these are "graphic elements in the public consciousness." (3) On the one hand, there is the suggestion that vivid pictures of the ways in which women are violated are present in the imagination and awareness of people. On the other hand, the persons responsible for the rape and violence (men) are not mentioned; the crimes are named but not the criminals. In another image, Clark describes women who are poor as "often inaudible . . . behind closed doors," and fears that they "will be invisible to the vast majority." (44) The scene conjured up with these metaphors is that of destitute women whose complaints cannot be heard outside their enclosures, and so, having no voice or visibility, they will not be noticed by the larger population.

Inviting his readers through metaphors to hear and respond to present day issues, Clark states that "we cannot try to turn back the clock to a time when today's questions did not exist." (2) He asserts that "a world speeding toward the twenty-first century poses questions about the stability of marriage, the relationship between spouses, and responsibility to and for children." (4) These are like other orientation metaphors which deal with time and space; they are dependent upon the frame of reference of the writer. In the first statement, the inexorability of today's questions is asserted next to the impossibility of winding the clock backward to another age. In the next metaphor the world (civilization) is imaged as whirling rapidly in space toward a future era, while present questions arise about the love and duties inherent in human relationships. For Clark, it is imperative that today's questions command our attention because their answers will shape our future in the next century.

In the above selection of metaphors which relate a "new consciousness" to experiences in today's culture, some patterns may be found. In general, the bishops attempt to deal with the social realities of U.S. culture affecting women, several of them situating the "new" consciousness of women's dignity within a universal context. Through a metaphoric process, some bishops venture a description of key elements of women's experience, such as their bonding with other women, their unequal and even disdainful treatment by society (men), their feelings of rejection and frustration, their experience of violence and poverty as well as role-stereotyping on the basis of their sex. The metaphors also reveal the negative ways in which women's new consciousness—like inflation—is experienced in society, and the fact that some people may want to return to another age when this issue was dormant. These are the issues the bishops identified through metaphor as those which society and the church must recognize and challenge.

## *Women and Culture: A Future Orientation*

Equality for women, held out as achievable at some future time, is treated as both an issue and a value in a variety of metaphorical images. Dozier envisions "the new age that is opening up as women are increasingly allowed full participation in all sectors of society" (6) and declares, "No woman is an island; every day she is being told: 'You are part of the mainland.' " (3) The image generated is open to several interpretations. On the one hand, women may be seen as taking their place in the totality of society, no longer isolated in their own separate activities—and this change signals a new age. On the other hand, the image suggests that woman is being incorporated into an already existing structure, perhaps even being absorbed into its form without making any changes in it.

Further metaphorical contributions to this future are found in the letter from the Minnesota bishops. They believe that "equality needs to be nourished by new models of participation" (12) and that, "as more and more women raise their own and society's consciousness of the dignity of women, a future of equality will be forged." (12) In the first statement, equality is given ontological status, something that must be fed in order to grow, and it is the new models of participation which will give it life. The second metaphor is a common one. *To raise consciousness* is to heighten awareness, a movement which suggests that elements in the recesses of one's consciousness (perhaps even located in the unconscious) need to be brought to one's awareness through new information, through the invitation to look at the elements in a new way, or through a new filter. The result is a further differentiation, a stretching to include what is "other" than the previously understood. The Minnesota bishops state unequivocally that the task of raising consciousness belongs to women themselves, and that the future will be *forged* through this activity. The use of *forge* here, (that is, "to hammer into shape while malleable with heat") renders a powerful image.

Three more metaphors which hint at some future era, and which invite probing, are found in the letters of Dozier and Maher. More complex than some, they draw the imagination into intriguing scenarios. Dozier writes, "salted by the intransigence of religious tradition, spiced with Americana and the greater expectations of our cultural conditions, we hardly recognize the greater criteria for authenticity and honesty which have surfaced today." (6) The subject of the sentence is "we" and, as subject, "we" are both salted and spiced. Salt and spice both pertain to food; the first is a mineral known as medicinal, as a preservative, and as piquant to the taste; the second is a vegetable known to be aromatic and give zest. The "salt" of our being is the refusal to compromise when it comes to our religious heritage, "salt" read here as both a preservative and as lending a piquant flavor. The "spices" of our being are unnamed American peculiarities and the awaited prospects of good fortune. The effect of this "seasoning," Dozier argues, has diminished our capacity to identify the standards of and make judgments about what is genuine.

In another dramatic and complex image, Dozier says:

> In this age, the long and subtle servitude begins to give way to the weight of justice where equality under the law can be asserted. Where the assurance of law holds no promise, it must be perceived that the woman of today will find security in the global solidarity of her international sorority. (3)

During the time of this writing (1975), debates about the Equal Rights Amendment abounded, and Dozier's insight into the power of the law to assure equality was probably related. He saw that women's servitude was only beginning to give way to the demands of justice, looking to equality under the law. Then, searching for a more secure image, he tried once again to describe women's bonding at an international level. However, his choice of metaphor is problematic. The phrase, "the global solidarity of her international sorority," is jarring because *sorority* is more easily related to carefree co-eds, bonded for pleasure and status on a university campus, than to the original Latin rendering of "sisterhood."

Maher also offers some complex metaphors in an exhortation toward the end of his pastoral. Writing of "the consumer mentality," he warns, "The society in which we live could become wedded to and crippled by utilitarianism. If women should wed this spirit of our age, they may soon be widowed." (10) The metaphor here is difficult to pursue, one of those a reader must follow with attention to the end of its function. There is action and movement in this sequence—and a revelation. One way to read it is to start with a key word, *utilitarianism,* a valuing of things and, perhaps, people for the sake of their usefulness. It suggests a self-interest that could develop into an unlimited materialism which always looks for something more. Metaphorically, society is imaged as crippled, when it is coupled with utilitarianism. (Here, imagine humankind with crutches.) But when women couple with the spirit of utilitarianism, they may find themselves without the generative power of their inner creative spirit (of which the masculine is a symbol) which is deadened through seeking fullness and completion by way of material goods. Read this way, the extended metaphor is exhortative. It encourages women not to be taken in by culture, but to be above culture. Note, however, that women are not encouraged to be a transforming element within it.

In sum, the metaphors which hint at some future era appear to hold ambiguities. They depict women as able to participate fully in the larger society, and then suggest that there should be new models of that participation which will develop society's understanding of equality. It is said to be women's task to conscientize others in a society which is characterized by an intransigent religious tradition and great expectations. Women's bonding with one another is seen as promising more security than possible changes in the law directed toward enforcing their equality. Finally, women are cautioned against the consumerism of our age. In my view, the mixture of images in this section reflects the ambiguity that men experience with regard to women's struggle for equality. On the one hand, it is necessary and desirous; on the other hand, there is much uncertainty about what that equality will look like, how it will affect society and women themselves, or how active a role women should take in creating it.

## *Women and Culture: Conclusion*

In the bishops' pastorals, the wide variety of metaphors which relate to the topic of "Women and Culture" kindle the imagination. They disclose obvious and increasingly subtle dimensions of woman's subordination to man in history, elements of women's heightened consciousness today, and the worldwide quest for equality. The reality of sexism and its contradiction to the gospel are acknowledged in some of these metaphors. Others depict women's experience of prejudice and dehumanizing treatment by society and also the ways in which women participate in the existing culture and structures of society that contribute to their exploitation. The cultural projection of "acceptable" feminine images, and woman's internalization of these limited views of both her identity and her potential, seem to be primary in reinforcing her subordination. Ambiguities about the women's movement are revealed in the metaphors, and there are only hints at what might be positive in a future age of equality in relationships.

It is interesting to note that there are no metaphors in the pastoral letters which describe the corresponding experience of men, who have held power and authority over women for centuries. Neither are there metaphors which embody the male experience of heightened consciousness with regard to women, nor the male's recognition that a future of equality will necessitate a relinquishing of privilege. It seems that the bishops have attempted to enter into and relate women's experience without depicting men's analogous experience. The absence of metaphors related to the male experience points to the basic structural contradiction of men's writing about women. It also reinforces the notion that the male experience is normative, and that it is the sub-normative that must be described.

## II. Women and the Church

In the twelve pastorals, metaphors which depict the role of women in the church encompass historical realities as well as tensions in the local church today. They also hint broadly at the direction in which the church is headed. Through metaphor, the bishops acknowledge the reality of tradition and structures in the church which have restricted women's participation and development as baptized persons.

The restrictions have had many consequences, many of which are reflected in metaphors. Jesus' teaching of mutuality and equality has not been heard within the church; the accretions of a patriarchal system have led to the identification of the church with the all-male hierarchy; the mission of the church has suffered; and there are women who experience alienation and anger. There are also metaphors which reflect some positive changes that have occurred in recent times. Women are being called to serve in a variety of ministries today, and some feel empowered by a new sense of responsibility for shaping the organization of the church, at least at the local level.

In the following section, metaphors within this theme are discussed from three perspectives: historical images, present day views, and prophetic images. The section ends with a short summary of the meanings which emerge in the exploration.

### *Women in the Church: Historical Images*

Metaphors that depict historical realities serve to interpret them in a fresh way. They can help us put past experience in perspective as well as illuminate contemporary experience. Through comparative images, they can reveal the stages between where we have been and where we are going. Sometimes a tension between the past and present can be observed, as in the following statement from Dozier's pastoral:

> Parish plants which once were the specific revelation of the Church's identity, concede to newer marks that are strangely feminine: welcome, friendship, love, hospitality, warmth.... This humanizing process leaves behind in history the scene of the representative clergy who had all the answers and symbolized the Catholic Church for the immigrant thousands. It leaves behind the political types who refashioned parochial boundaries into political wards and stamped official ecclesial existence with the indelible mark of a male domain. (5)

In Dozier's extended metaphor, the signs and identity of the church in previous decades are contrasted with the signs and identity of the church today. In the first sentence, parish plants, once seen as synonymous with church, are given ontological status: they "yield" to the recent developments described as "newer marks" (reminiscent of the "four marks of the church"). Those "marks" Dozier identifies as "strangely feminine," that is, of woman and, therefore, unfamiliar or at least surprisingly different from "the indelible mark of a male domain" referred to later. Throughout the entire statement, which may be read as an extended metaphor, these two kinds of "marks" are held in tension.

Dozier names the feminine contribution a "humanizing process." He says it has supplanted or replaced ("left behind in history") the familiar setting of clerics who had all the answers, some of whom were political types who saw parish organizations as potential political entities. Although Dozier asserts that the *newer marks* have displaced the old, the final phrase suggests that the official church is invincibly masculine. It has been *stamped* with the *indelible marks of a male domain.* Dozier's point seems to be that newer marks, effected in the humanizing process of hospitality, warmth, welcome and friendship, have made male supremacy at the local level seem like past history, but not in the realm of the official church. With this extended metaphor, Dozier situates today's church as existing in the tension between the male dominated past and the mutuality of male/female relationships which is not yet a reality.

Another metaphorical statement hearkens back to the early church community which thrived on mutuality in relationships during the thirty years following Jesus' resurrection. Gerety, whose pastoral abounds in metaphors for the church (pilgrim church, a community in Christ, the body of Christ, the new creation, local church, universal church), wants us to find "the true face of the church." He asserts that it is "[women's] role in the church today which is of supreme importance . . . for the rediscovery by believers of the true face of the church." (11) By this metaphor Gerety suggests that the outward expression of the body of Christ has not yet achieved its authentic aspect and will not until the question of women's role is dealt with—a task of "supreme importance" for believers, not one to be taken lightly. If the "true face of the church" has not yet been uncovered by believers today, they are living with but a partial view. Hence the imperative to deal with the question.

Because of the word *rediscovery,* this metaphor reaches back to days of the early church when women's broad participation in the church enabled them to live the gospel message more fully. For example, Magdalene, Priscilla, Junia, and Phoebe served as preachers, organizers, leaders of house churches, or deaconesses. Rosemary Ruether makes the point that women's ministry in the early church cannot be seen as "an irregular accident but rather the expression of an alternative world-view."[7] From my perspective, Gerety deserves credit for supporting the view that today's male-dominated church structures are a distorted development of the early church community which more truly reflected the equality and mutuality of the sexes in its ministry.

Another metaphor for the church might be described as orientational. It contrasts past images with present day insights and situates the reader through a rhetorical question. In Weakland's task force report the question is asked: "Can the Church be a leader in society with regard to women or will the Church always follow society?" (3A) The question is posed with two images of the church, one as the people of God out in front, leading the way, and the other as lagging behind the masses of society. The inference is that historically the church has taken its cues from society and the cultural forces that shape it. In the question that is posed, however, the church is urged to make a choice. Read in the light of today's teaching on social justice, the church's clear mission in the face of injustice is to lead the way by example and by teaching.

We can gain historical perspective from the metaphors discussed above. The pre-Vatican II, male-dominated parish structures come readily to mind. We are also invited to consider the role of ministry in the early church, when women's participation was less restricted, to rediscover Christ's desires for his church. Finally, we gain understanding of the church's role of leadership in relation to society. Taken together, these images give a picture of the church aligned so closely with the patriarchal structures and direction of society that it has lost its "true face"—that is, its authentic reflection of Jesus Christ. Yet there is also a note of hope in the metaphors. Our search for women's role today can help us rediscover Christ's original intent. A feminine humanizing process has already begun

---

[7] Rosemary Radford Ruether, *Disputed Questions: On Being a Christian* (Nashville: Abingdon, 1982), p. 123.

to affect the church, and our discussion of women's rightful place may be an impetus for the church to assert its authority and lead the way in shaping a future of equality of persons.

## *Women and the Church: Present Day Views*

Prolific images depict women's role and experience in today's church. Some bishops describe the mission of women today in elevated terms, while some take a pastoral approach toward those women who feel alienated from the church. One image portrays a bishop's purpose in a decision he made prohibiting lay (women) homilists at the liturgy. Several metaphors offer women's own insights into their experience in today's church. This variety of metaphors is explored in the following paragraphs.

The first of the pastorals presents a high ideal for woman. Maher states that "Endowed with God-given faith, hope and love, in the assurance of their identity and purpose, women of the new world should indeed exert unprecedented power and influence to restore this universe to the state of peace and harmony cardinal to the divine plan for mankind [sic]." (13) This lofty, metaphoric vision suggests that there are women all over the world who have not only the mission to restore peace to the world and universe but the self-assurance to accomplish it. When the bishop ascribes to women the actuality of "unprecedented power and influence" he hearkens back to the nineteenth century ideal of true womanhood—that women are the moral arm of the universe. He holds out a goal that is distant and idealistic and realistically unachievable in the order of time.

Similarly, Dozier takes up the universal dimension of women's ministry and its missionary aspect. In a metaphor that reaches around the globe, he writes that "there is no doubt that the universal woman is one of the great effective and credible transmitters of the Gospel. She goes into every nation beholding the presence of the Lord with her." (4) Further on he says, "In seeking new ways to energize and transmit the Gospel, all of us must look to its most ready and apt media: the liberated Christian woman." (4) In naming *the universal woman* and *the liberated woman* Dozier seeks to identify a quality or call of each woman. But his entire statement is neither prescriptive nor descriptive; instead, he offers us a romantic view of this woman who communicates the good news/presence of the Lord as she travels to every nation.

Maher's and Dozier's statements, with their images of women either accomplishing mighty deeds or achieving a luminous, mystical state in their discipleship, can be read as a retreat from women's stated issues and the daily reality. The vision presented in both statements inspires neither the bishops nor women to concrete action. One way of backing off from the concrete day-to-day reality of women's oppression and the bedrock question of inequality is to keep looking up and beyond to idealistic images.

In contrast, several bishops mention women's experience of anger and/or alienation and take a pastoral approach. In one statement, the Minnesota bishops write, "Our pastoral concern goes out to all women in pain and alienation, to the woman alienated from religion . . . the woman who hears God's call to serve through a variety of ministries or leadership positions but is blocked by tradition." (12) The image here is one of the bishops reaching out with solicitude toward women who have either turned away from the institutional church and who suffer dislocation, or who bear the pain of interference when, desirous of responding to God's call to serve, they find themselves blocked by tradition. The verbs in the statement carry the metaphoric action: the *concern goes out,* that is, a sympathetic reaching out to understand the pain; *the woman alienated from religion,* that is, estranged or disjoined from that which is key to her personhood; the woman *who hears but is blocked,* that is, who understands her vocation as a baptized person in the church and who is ready to live it fully but is obstructed from doing so. Tradition, rather than those who rigidly uphold it, is identified as the obstacle.

Gerety writes with similar pastoral concern: "Let us understand with compassion the legitimate anger on the part of some women toward those structures or traditions which have demanded and expected less than full priesthood from them." (2) The image here is of the bishop calling upon the local church community to understand and care for those women whose anger toward structures or traditions is valid (or lawful, or logically correct). In the metaphor, the structures and traditions are personified as not having asked full priesthood of women, suggesting that they are responsible for limiting to the male half of the human race the role of mediation between God and the laity. While Gerety addresses the issue of legitimate anger, his metaphorical language here serves to distance the anger from its real cause. In addition, by naming the "structures" as the cause of women's anger, the metaphor hides the identity of the decision-makers responsible for the unjust structures.

Gerety ventures another metaphorical statement to describe what the church is asking of women today. He says, "In our time the Church clearly desires that women should become aware of the greatness of their mission and take their equal, if sometimes different, place alongside their brothers in Christ." (11) The church here may be understood in the inclusive sense, that is, the laity and hierarchy. This church is depicted as desiring a change in that women should not hold back but step forward and take their equal place with men, their brothers in Christ. The image is one of men and women standing together side by side, ready to serve as equals. However, the qualification given: "equal, if sometimes different" is what stands out. Suddenly the image crumbles; men and women no longer stand on the same ground as equals. The qualifier, *if sometimes different*, conjures up arbitrary restrictions that render women's role subordinate.

A central question needs to be entertained here. Is there possibility for true equality under the axiom "Equal, if sometimes different"? It reads like a restatement of an old racist ideal: "Separate but equal." This ideal has already been arbitrated by the civil rights legislation which declared that "separate but equal" is inherently unjust. The reason is that "separate" is always determined by the dominant group and the subordinate group always carries a stigma. Thus, a close reading of the statement about what "the Church clearly desires" shows it to be sexist because the "sometimes different place" serves to ratify male domination.

In his lengthy pastoral, Clark deals with both larger philosophical issues and the concrete particulars related to women's role in the church today. Like Gerety, he has many metaphors for the church; among the most often used is "a pilgrim church" which Clark explains is a still imperfect, learning church. He brings up the sensitive issue of lay preaching during the mass and refers to a previous directive he had made that "only ordained persons should preach the homily at the Eucharistic liturgy. . . ." He writes that his "intention was then and is now to be in concert with the whole college of bishops. . . ." (66) The metaphor *to be in concert with the whole college of bishops* suggests the solidarity and unified approach the bishops want in their governance of the U.S. Catholic church. It also expresses the pull—and normally deciding factor—that bishops experience when an anomaly in church practice at the local level must be reviewed. For those among the laity who must live with a decision they disagree with, the metaphor might highlight their feeling of powerlessness and frustration in trying to bring about needed changes.

A metaphor in the pastoral from Milwaukee, prepared by the task force which listened to women all over the archdiocese, is striking for its sense of the concrete and ordinary, and in its contrast to the above statements. For example, the writers assert that "In many cases, it seems, women are expected to make coffee while men make decisions. Women who do not abide by that expectation are frequently criticized by men and women alike." (4A) The analogy in the first sentence between making decisions and making coffee evokes an image of men meeting together in an enclosed room and women standing outside measuring the water for the coffee pot, probably to serve the men at their meeting. This scene is the kind that provides apt material for the cartoonist and grist for women's anger in their experience of being underrepresented in, and more often excluded from, discussion about the direction of church affairs. Too often it is only men who make decisions for them, assuming that women's place is secondary. The metaphor captures a scene from the concrete day-to-day reality.

In summary, some apt points can be derived from the above selection of metaphors on the role of women in the church today. The bishops recognize both the pain of the alienated, disillusioned women as well as the potential of the liberated, empowered women. The bishops try to keep in view the mission of the church today while some of their metaphors reveal what women may recognize as inconsistent. For example, the bishops speak of the church's desire that women share fully Christ's mission and at the same time reinforce woman's "different" role which the male hierarchy reserves the right to define. They address the angry and the alienated with pastoral concern, and they envisage a universal mission for women who are impelled by the message of the gospel. This mixture of images is not unlike those in other groupings. The strong encouragement to women to remain active in the church, when joined with a reinforcement of the traditional restrictions, continues to be a source of frustration for women.

## Women and the Church: Prophetic Images

Among a possible fifteen metaphors which have a prophetic or future dimension, five qualify for study here. These are representative and dominant metaphors, fruitful to unpack. They point to the future and help us name where the Spirit is prodding us in the here and now. Some bishops, like Dozier, begin with the concrete. He offers us a metaphoric vision in the following statement:

> There is a sinful condition of apathy and indifference in secular and Church life. We find apathy among Christians when believers stop growing in maturity in Christ. Part of the reason might be, as far as woman is concerned, that the woman no longer fits the traditional ecclesial role she inherited. She is not enthusiastic about a condition that has not kept pace with her life's experience. She might even be depressed by the realization that no one really cares. Yet the Church needs her gift, the Church needs the Christian woman in an ecclesial role that enriches her life and the life of her Church community with Christian vitality. (6)

In this extended metaphor, Dozier explores a new way of seeing an existing condition. He tries to probe a particular situation he has observed: apathy and indifference on the part of women in relation to the possibilities of their participation in the life of the church. Woman, he says, "no longer fits" her inherited role in the church; while her life experience has taken her beyond it and she is ready to serve in a greater capacity, she may sense only indifference from others. Dozier's vision sets the scene for the institutional church to take the next step. He recognizes that woman needs the church and the church needs her—but only "in an ecclesial role that enriches her life and the life of her Church community with Christian vitality." Dozier apparently sees the connection between structures that foster an expression of one's full personhood and a vital community where gifts are freely exercised.

Clark, writing more than seven years later, touches on more of the particulars:

> We cannot ignore [women's] absence from advisory or decision-making bodies or positions; nor can we justify it on the grounds of their inexperience in certain kinds of Church affairs or their lack of certain skills. Such attempts at justification will create a circle of self-fulfilling prophecies which will continue to keep many qualified women at the periphery of Church affairs. (88)

The metaphors of "the circle of self-fulfilling prophecies" and "women at the periphery of Church affairs" may stir the complacent. The first phrase suggests that prejudices against women, thought to be unqualified or incompetent to participate in the very decisions which affect their lives and that of the church community, still prevail. The second part depicts women's place on the outer edge of decision-making circles, unrelated to the center or source of church life. In this statement, Clark addresses structural obstacles, as well as unfounded arguments against inclusion, that women face in seeking participation in the life of the church. He both acknowledges women's invisibility in leadership positions and cuts through the kind of rationalization that prevents women from further inclusion.

Likewise, Hunthausen points out the structural problem in his pastoral letter. He asserts that "we continue to look critically at existing structures, to discern whether they foster or hinder full personhood of women and men in the Church." (4) Twice in the pastoral he refers to Catherine of Siena, known for her obedience to legal church authority but also for challenging popes to face the structural issues of their day. He wants structures which will "foster . . . full personhood." By personifying "structures" as having power to nourish (or prevent) personal growth, Hunthausen touches on a critical point of the issues today. For the hierarchical structures of the church, which allow only ordained men in positions of governance and teaching authority, effectively keep women from those expressions of personhood.

Finally, let us consider metaphors which point to the way change is occurring within the church. The first is from Weakland's task force report. In summarizing the changing perceptions and roles of women in society and church, the task force refers to a change in theological vision emanating from Vatican II. This new vision emphasized the church as the people of God, a community based in the sacrament of baptism, a change which initiated a new age for women in the U.S. Catholic Church. The conception of church as primarily institutional, and as identified with the all-male hierarchy, no longer held sway.

> Women listen keenly as the Church insists on the equality and dignity of all human persons. Some for the first time are learning the import and responsibility of their baptism. They are beginning to regard their talents as gifts given by God and, in a spirit of responsible stewardship, they look for roles wherein these gifts might best be used. *The view of women as working for the Church is giving way to a new self-perception in which women view themselves as being the Church in service of others.* Where this perception has taken hold, women are assuming a sense of responsibility for shaping the organization of the Church. (3A) (Italics added)

This long quotation provides context to the metaphor (italicized) that is discussed. The first part, "the view of women as working for the Church," is an objective perspective. It suggests separateness and subordination. One might think of women washing the altar linens. This "view" is given ontological status with the verbal phrase, "is giving way"; the old view yields its predominance to "a new self-perception," one that is subjective. In this perspective, women appropriate their own sense of church in their service of others; they identify with Jesus Christ's mission in the world. A further analogy suggests itself. Women, in identifying with the church, see themselves as incorporated in Christ.

Mahony also offers us an image of church today as in a period of transition. He writes of the tensions experienced over the role of women, and calls his people to face them "and whatever reforms they may call us to." As if addressing groups which have formed their own worship communities, he pleads for patience and communion in resisting the temptation "to split off." Desirous of keeping his flock unified, he warns:

> There is no salvation without incarnation. The Church only grows from within, and our ministry to one another is this mutual ministry of support, correction, and love. (3)

Mahony's image, "the Church only grows from within," suggests the powerful effect of relationships in the church. Immediately after, he suggests a way to the growth desired: a "mutual ministry of support, correction and love." By calling for *mutual ministry* Mahony encourages strong adult relationships which exclude whatever rings of paternalism or childish dependence. To choose not to "split off," he suggests, is to be called to relate in an adult ministry to one another within the present structures.

The encouraging note in the metaphors discussed above is that *tradition* and the *existing structures* of the church are identified as the cause of women's discouragement, along with the call to look critically at both causes and to move beyond "the circle of self-fulfilling prophecies." It is evident in these metaphorical statements that new forms of presence and witness are available to the Christian community amid the very structures in need of change. The difference in images from 1975 (Dozier: "woman no longer fits the ecclesial role she inherited") to 1982 (Weakland's task force report: "women view themselves as being the Church in service of others") is also a hopeful sign. It indicates that newly developed areas for pastoral activity and theological reflection have increased the participation and contribution of the laity. The metaphors discussed are sputtering efforts at systemic change, however, for women's lack of political voice and consequent experience of powerlessness within church structures are not addressed.

### *Women and the Church: Conclusion*

Through the metaphors in their letters, the bishops image how changes have affected the local church, women themselves, and the wider church. What first strikes the reader is that many ambiguities exist. For while maintaining a traditional position about women's role, the bishops write in metaphors which indicate an open door into the future, a willingness to acknowledge that we have not yet seen the dimension of growth in women or the church which Christ intends. A few metaphors carry on the ideological propagandizing characteristic of another age, while there are several which address the question of change in church structures, such as the question of ordaining women to the priesthood. This collection of metaphors represents the nascent stages of the hierarchy's effort to probe today's questions and seek new answers.

It is of further interest to note that three metaphors in this section render men's experience as it relates to women in the church. Dozier depicts the "scene of the representative clergy" in times past. Clark speaks of his desire "to be in concert with the whole college of bishops." Weakland's task force reports that "women are expected to make coffee while men make decisions." The images in these statements, however, fail to reveal the male experience of heightened consciousness with regard to women; rather, they reinforce a view of male solidarity in a church which resists the full inclusion of women.

## III. Women and Men

While there are fewer metaphors for discussion in this category, there is no pastoral which does not take up the question of male-female relationship. Its utmost importance is stressed again and again. Maher, for example, refers to it as "the relationship which foreshadows all human relationships." (7) Other bishops probe the mystery of sexuality as it is related to the call of men and women to serve the church. Gerety, for example, writes of "partners in the mission of Christ." (9) Others emphasize the notion of complementarity. In two of the pastorals, sexual differences are explored in some detail from psychological and sociological viewpoints. Finally, in one pastoral the evil of sexism is probed (along with an examination of conscience on one's sexist attitudes) and the power of metaphorical God-language is recognized.

While the metaphors discussed below do not adequately represent the more complete treatment of the issues as they are developed in the pastorals, they do provide a framework for discussion of some basic views of the bishops toward sexuality and toward gender differences that affect women's designated "place" and role in the church. The discussion is organized in the following way. First, those metaphors will be explored which image the notion of *complementarity* as a God-given principle for male/female relationships. Second, the metaphors related to the issue of sexism will be discussed. Finally, those metaphors whose heuristic power can help us move from the known to an unknown, to a future time of equal partnership, will be unpacked.

## *Men and Women: Complementarity*

Because the idea of complementarity is fundamental to many bishops' understanding of the ideal relationship between the sexes, an exploration of its meaning is included here. This will help us understand the theological cast this notion is given in the pastorals and the metaphors related to it. The fullest description is given in the pastoral of the Minnesota bishops who explain that "the notion [of complementarity] shall be an underlying principle" in their reflections. First of all, they stress the equal dignity of women and men. Then they refer to creation accounts and Jesus' reference to them, which "leave no doubt that there are differences, beyond the merely biological, between women and men—differences not negated even by baptismal incorporation into Christ." They continue:

> These differences are intrinsic to God's basic purpose in creation, for man and woman in close partnership were given the responsibility to beget and to rear children and to exercise authority, in God's stead, over all the rest of creation. Arising out of these differences come certain principles which affect the relationships between women and men. One of the most important of these is that of complementarity. Woman complements man—physically, spiritually, and psychologically; man complements woman in the same ways. This notion shall be an underlying principle in these reflections. (15)

The line of thinking represented here is compatible with that of the other bishops who employ the notion of *complementarity*. When this notion is emphasized, so are the differences between men and women—in their sexuality, in their gifts of ministry, in their ways of imaging God. The articulation of the particular aspects of complementarity, however, can cause difficulties in interpretation. The problems arise less because of sexual (biological) differences than because of gender (culturally conditioned) differences.

From the outset, Maher sets the theme of complementarity as part of God's blueprint for humanity:

> In the divine design, men and women are meant to complement each other, to enhance and affirm each other as persons, knowing perfect trust and mutuality. Their relationship foreshadows all human relationships and mirrors the inter-rela-

tedness of the Persons of the Blessed Trinity. They are the expression of a divine harmony in diversity. (7)

"The divine design" is a metaphor for God's original plan or intention. The relationship of complementarity is described in such idealistic terms as one of "perfect trust and mutuality," and metaphorically as being a harbinger for other human relationships. Finally, Maher says, it "mirrors," that is, gives a true picture of the trinitarian relationship. The language of this discourse is appropriate to the most sublime theology. All reality has a sacramental dimension and function: to speak of God, to evoke God, to point to God. And God has created difference—in this case, the masculine and the feminine—"in order to communicate to that difference."[8] Maher's metaphorical statement touches on the mystery of sexual differences and its heuristic function in the sense that in these differences we detect the ultimate will of God.

A further aspect of complementarity is delineated in one of Dozier's metaphorical statements. He says, "Neither men nor women will come to full personhood in a society where the gifts of one or the other are suppressed. 'Male and female, God created them' and their complementary interaction and development brings each to maturity." (6) "Gifts" in this passage refers to one's particular talents or personal characteristics that contribute to the development of creation. "Suppressed," a verb which connotes physical restraint, can also mean *abolish*. In the metaphor, Dozier asserts that where a person's gifts are suppressed, full personhood (maturity) is not possible. Gifts flourish where there is "complementary interaction" and human development along the lines of sexual differences.

---

[8] Leonardo Boff, OSM, *The Maternal Face of God: The Feminine and Its Religious Expressions*, p. 91. He asserts that "The very existence of human beings as masculine and feminine finds its *raison d'être* in their potential to be receptacles of God."

In effect, Dozier's extended metaphor suggests that the maturity of each person is dependent upon the complementary interaction of male and female.

Finally, the Minnesota bishops, already quoted at length above, add still another aspect to the notion of complementarity. They assert that parents' own self-fulfillment and the spiritual, psychological, and emotional fulfillment of their children "will happen if they maintain that clear complementarity between them which involves their whole being and flows from the fact that 'male and female he created them.' (Gen. 1 and 2)" (16) Here, *complementarity* is metaphorically depicted as something that can be maintained—that is, preserved, or provided for. It is depicted as a way of relating which involves each person's "whole being" and which "flows" from the reality of having been created male or female. This statement suggests an understanding of complementarity as a way of relating to one another out of distinct differences which issue from one's sexual identity.

Because it is described in general terms rather than in particular ones, the notion of *complementarity* in the three metaphors discussed above can be understood in terms of mutuality and not role definitions. However, the language of *complementarity* can reduce human beings to their differences. It is predicated on incompleteness, on fragmentation, whereas the preferred term *mutuality* is predicated on wholeness and the full development of the person. The use of *complementarity* to describe the desired relationship between men and women is also problematic because those who approve its scheme are those who enjoy privileged status. When complementarity is used to suggest that women are superior to men, it only masks the reality of dependency. Finally, to the extent that *complementarity* means "equal, but different" and is promoted as a norm, a theology that assumes male standards of normative humanity remains in place.

## Women and Men: Issues of Sexism

Many of the bishops address the issue of sexism, defined very powerfully in one pastoral as grievously sinful.

> Sexism, directly opposed to Christian humanism and feminism, is the erroneous belief or conviction or attitude that one sex, female or male, is superior to the other in the very order of creation or by the very nature of things. When anyone believes that men are inherently superior to women or that women are inherently superior to men, then he or she is guilty of sexism. Sexism is a moral and social evil. It is not the truth of the biological, sociological or psychological sciences, nor is it the truth of the Gospel. Sexism is a lie. It is a grievous sin, diminished in its gravity only by indeliberate ignorance or by pathological fear. (Balke and Lucker: 3)

The sinfulness of sexism is addressed in this pastoral alone. Elsewhere it is treated as a cultural condition which oppresses and is unjust, and metaphors are used to describe its origin and its cost. In Maher's pastoral, for example, it is described as the human rebellion against God and God's plan, which forms the basis for interpreting the dualism in male/female relationships. He says: "With the fall from grace, mankind [sic] set their hearts against God (Gen 6:5) and the urge to attain and exert superiority over one another to dominate and subjugate came to possess all beings." (7) The familiar root metaphors, "the fall from grace" and "set their hearts against God," tell the Judaeo-Christian story of sin entering the world and its consequences for humankind. The "fall from grace" indicates a breach in a relationship, a failure to hold up one's part in a contract or bond, thereby losing out on supernatural help. The interior determination on humanity's part to live out that breach or failure is described as a decision to "set their hearts against God," a metaphor for choosing feelings of

## Metaphors in the Pastorals

alienation. The urge to dominate and subjugate another was an outgrowth of the experience of alienation. Thus Maher offers one basis for sexism.

Another basis, according to Maher, may be found in cultural conditioning which had its beginnings in primitive societies, where, "by nature of her biological processes," woman's activities were curtailed:

> In her circumscribed world, a woman's work was largely individual and of limited authority. Man, on the other hand, was perforce drawn into group action, wars and protective councils, which necessitated direction and the recognition of leadership. Since recorded time, leadership—with some exceptions—has been assumed as a male prerogative. (7)

In delineating the differences between the two "worlds," one limited within certain boundaries, the other unrestrained and ever-expanding, the extended metaphor employs two key verbs. A woman's world *was circumscribed* —probably not by her. Man *was drawn into* his work; leadership *has been assumed* to be a male prerogative. The latter two verbs are passive, turning the responsibility for the action away from the male. The first of these describes a kind of magnetic force which pulls the male outward. The second describes a consequence of men's experience. It is important to note further the difference in describing the two worlds of women and men: the first is indicated in the singular: *a woman's work;* the second is indicated in the plural: *man drawn into group action.* Maher's metaphor depicts the assumption of power by men in their experience of male solidarity in contrast to the subordinate role assigned to women, whose work kept them separate from one another. The group in power maintains a view of superiority, based on sex, over/against the individuals who are subordinate. In this statement,

Maher's use of passive language implies that no one is responsible. His language accentuates the subordination of women.

Another metaphor where the language reinforces the practice of male domination is found in Balke and Lucker's pastoral. Taking a psychological perspective, they identify "costs" of sexism for both male and female as very different:

> For women, the psychological costs of sexism are indeed extremely high; the tendency toward psychological paralysis, disabling them from asserting their self-worth. For men, the costs of sexism are also high; they are victimized by hyper-rationalism, by an underdeveloped affective life, by the need to dominate and control. (3)

With the words *paralysis* and *disabling*, the first statement leads the reader to image women as lame persons, unable to function normally. Their crippled state affects their ability to claim and defend their value as persons. With the word *victimized*, the second statement leads the reader to image men as overpowered by stronger force. One may applaud the attempt to balance the "psychological costs of sexism" as having adverse effects for both women and men. It must be noted also, however, that in this statement the use of the passive voice with regard to men relieves them of their responsibility for sexist behavior.

The three metaphors discussed above trace the bishops' views of the history of sexism to humankind's beginnings, give us a theological interpretation of the origin of sexism, and provide a psychological perspective on sexism's effect on women and men today. Through metaphors, some bishops have tried to open up the root sin of oppressive dualism which has been the basis for the long history of crimes against women. Their use of the passive voice, however, relieves men of the responsibility for the systematic oppression of women.

### Women and Men: Partners in Mission

The metaphors in this section are disappointingly few and comparatively unimaginative. They reinforce, in theory, the mutuality that women and men are called to achieve, but they do not help us envision what a full partnership will look like. Gerety is perhaps the most specific when he says:

> As partners in the mission of Christ, men and women are called to a ministry of shared responsibility, where the special gifts, talents and competencies of each are harmoniously activated in complementarity and mutuality. (9)

"Partners" may be read as a metaphor which calls up an association of equals, bonded for a particular purpose. In this instance, men and women are designated as partners who have shared responsibility in their ministry.

The metaphor is continued in the verbal phrase, where Gerety asserts that each one's special gifts, talents, and competencies *are harmoniously activated in complementarity and mutuality.* It is when men and women have shared responsibility for ministry that their gifts are activated. Here, Gerety points the way toward an alternative reality characterized by harmony. He prepares us for the day when women and men are truly partners and invites us to imagine capacities for mutuality that men possess as well as women. The key metaphor is "partners in mission," an image that suggests non-hierarchical relationships. As a designation for male/female relationship, it is a presentiment for the kind of mutuality that Christ wanted for his church.

Mahony offers two metaphors for the relationship of women and men. Like Gerety, he uses the image of *partners* to indicate a desirable relationship between men and women: "Women ... wish to join with men as partners in the task of working to bring about the Kingdom of justice and peace. . . ." (2) Here, Mahony is stating the desire of the women who participated in the archdiocesan consultation process. Later in the document, he writes that "we need to recover a greater sense of men and women working collaboratively, side by side." (3) In this statement, Mahony indicates that collaboration characterized the relationship in former times, and that collaboration means *side by side*—an image of two or more people standing/working together, looking out at the same horizon.

In another pastoral, Hunthausen draws our attention to the unity that exists between women and men. He asserts that "Solidarity marks the sexes." (2) *Solidarity* calls up an image of Lech Walesa and his labor union in Poland, or protestors in a demonstration where the communion of interests is evidenced in raised fists or a march or joined hands. To be in solidarity is to defy anyone or anything to break a union. When solidarity "marks" something as a visible sign, it is conspicuous. For Hunthausen, the mark of solidarity in this passage designates unity, a theme he continues to explore:

> The beautiful Song of Songs portrays man and woman in mutual harmony after the fall; love is the meaning of their life, a love that excludes oppression and exploitation. Sexual love expands existence beyond the stereotypes of society—no male dominance, no female subordination, no stereotyping of either sex. (2)

Here, Hunthausen tries to express the solidarity that sexual love can achieve. He describes it as a relationship of "mutual harmony" and says "it expands existence beyond the stereotypes"; here is an "orientation" metaphor which emerges from an experience of space and our capacity for movement through space. Hunthausen holds up the ideal relationship represented in the Song of Songs: that to feel one's existence expanded through the experience of sexual love is to know one's existence beyond culturally induced differences.

Finally, the Minnesota bishops identify the challenge ahead. They say, "The task before us is how to bring that day nearer when full partnership will be a reality and when inevitable sacrifices will be shared together." (12) This is another orientation metaphor, following on the human tendency to see the future as up ahead. Time and space are described here in the metaphoric phrase "how to bring that day nearer"—an attempt to correlate today's task with an unknown time in the future. Our concrete task is metaphorically depicted as making the vision of an alternative future a reality.

In this section we have explored in idealized presentations themes of full partnership, of complementarity and mutuality, of collaboration, of solidarity and sexual love which go beyond sexual stereotypes. Our task of making the future a reality is also depicted metaphorically in the discussion of women and men as partners, working together side by side, in Christ's mission. Here, a critical point emerges. While the metaphors portray an underlying reality and a long-range goal, even a shift to an egalitarian concept which challenges the "naturalness" of hierarchical social structures, they do not point to a vision of social reconstruction that expresses liberation from sexism. If a vision of equality does not also include the basis for change, it will turn out to be a mirage and women's sense of defeat will be augmented.

## *Women and Men: Conclusion*

The metaphors studied above reveal three key points —first of all, the ideology of complementarity that prevails in the hierarchical church. The experience of those (women) whose complementary role is defined by others (male hierarchy), however, is that the notion of complementarity too often becomes a matter of role compromise. Those who are compromised and kept in place are already marginal to the dominant consensus.

Secondly, the metaphors related to the problem of sexism look for their content in the human experience of alienation from God after the fall, and in social roles along the lines of division of labor. These metaphors indicate that sexism is not seen as biologically inevitable. Neither is sexism depicted as the expression of unconscious forces. In two pastorals, its grievously sinful nature is recognized; only one pastoral suggests the need to repent this sin in history. Nowhere else is there outrage expressed at the pervasive abuse of women, physically and psychologically violent abuse, which continues in our own time.

Finally, the metaphors portray an ideal of "partnership" and "solidarity" for women and men as they work "side by side." The ideal, however, remains only a romantic vision of God's plan for us unless, at the same time, we recognize the social reconstruction necessary in the church for its concretization. The metaphors do not suggest this element. Although feminist theology has articulated it, at depth and with eloquence, metaphors related to the necessary changes have not yet permeated the collective consciousness. We need images which can be catalysts for reconstruction and must listen to those who struggle for liberation to spawn them.[9]

## IV. Conversion and Reconciliation

Throughout the twelve pastorals, the clarion call to conversion and reconciliation indicates the bishops' desire

---

[9] See, for instance, Elisabeth Moltmann-Wendel, *A Land Flowing with Milk and Honey: Perspectives on Feminist Theology*, trans. by John Bowden (New York: Crossroad, 1986). The author explores images of God in the Christian tradition which make possible new total conceptions of life: wisdom (Sophia), Shekinah and Holy Spirit, and the non-patriarchal Father. See also Virginia Ramey Mollenkott, *The Divine Feminine: The Biblical Imagery of God as Female* (New York: Crossroad, 1986) and Susan Cady, *Sophia: The Future of Feminist Spirituality* (San Francisco: Harper and Row, 1986).

## Metaphors in the Pastorals

to activate the healing and liberating grace of the Christian faith. In this section, some metaphors are explored in order to clarify the healing and liberating words of the bishops and to flesh out their suggestions for that new church which women and men are asked to embody. The metaphors in this section are straightforward and undramatic. At times a familiar biblical ring can be heard. They reveal to us a basic stance some bishops have taken today with regard to a future church where women and men are called together to a full participation in the mission of Christ. In the discussion below, we consider four metaphors which summon us to conversion and three metaphors which illuminate the task of achieving reconciliation today.

Buswell situates our need for conversion in the context of the church's identity with the powerful in history, an identity which led the socially oppressed to become the victims of racism and sexism within the church. He writes: "We must work together to reverse this trend, and return to the early Christian ideal of true equality among all persons." (2) To *reverse the trend* signifies a turn in the opposite direction or position—in other words, turn around. *Return to the early Christian ideal* also implies a direction, to go back, retrace one's steps to a former position. In both phrases calling for conversion, Buswell would turn us around. He would head us back to the church's New Testament foundations and to a time prior to the accommodation of Christianity to patriarchy. In "the early Christian ideal" relationships were not rigidly patterned by dominance/subservience norms but were characterized by mutuality and service of one another.

In another pastoral, Gerety writes: "As we preach Christ to the world, we must undergo conversion and put our own household of faith in order." (2) Conversion, literally, means "change to a new form." Gerety states that conversion is something we must "undergo." This metaphor proclaims a necessary asceticism, asserting that we must submit ourselves to the process of changing to a new form. The command "we must" indicates that it is a choice we cannot fail to make. The last part of the metaphor, *put our own household of faith in order,* indicates an explicit task related to the process of conversion. The church as the household of faith is in disarray. That which is disordered must be put in place in the light of the change.

Not to be missed is the context for the conversion and task of reordering. The context is critical. It is our witness to the gospel: "As we preach Christ to the world." Gerety makes the point that the credibility of the Christian witness to the gospel necessitates our radical change and attention to social and personal relationships in the infrastructure of the church. I read Gerety's metaphor this way: because "there does not exist among you Jew or Greek, slave or free, male or female . . ." then in Christ's *household of faith* we must reorder our social and personal relationships to patterns of equal partnership.

Weakland, in his introduction to the task force report, envisions some of the particulars of conversion. He writes:

> We are being asked to stretch our horizons a bit. We are being asked to let go of stereotypes. We are being asked to search out what following Christ together as men and women really means. (1)

The three verbs in this statement carry the metaphorical images: *stretch, let go,* and *search out.* Weakland asserts that we are being asked to do each of these. The metaphor "stretch our horizons" captures the elastic-like tension inherent in changing one's perspective or viewpoint. A person's way of seeing the world shifts when something new is learned, whether from viewing the valley from the mountaintop or from gaining an insight into one's own limited understanding of truth. *Let go of stereotypes* is another metaphor for broadening one's perspective, but it is more particular. Stereotypes are the result of pre-judgment, a lack of openness to growing in knowledge and understanding of someone or something. To "let go" or shed stereotypes is one of the most demanding tasks a person can

## Metaphors in the Pastorals 93

undertake; it requires humility and a willingness to give up a perspective which allows one to feel power over another. *To search out* may be read as a metaphor suggesting a process of investigating, of careful exploring. Its meaning is less to look for something that is lost than to look for something yet to be discovered. Conversion, for Weakland, involves these three dimensions: shifting one's worldview, recognizing and rejecting stereotypes, and exploring a new way of being.

For Hunthausen also, conversion is a call to something new. He writes:

> Conversion is the process each must undergo in becoming the new person through faith and baptism. A new version of Church, a renewed sense of mission and community, impel each and every person to inquire: what does a Church look like that is whole, just, and moving toward full incarnation of the kingdom? (3)

Here again, conversion is seen as a "process" and something to which we must submit. In phrases similar to Weakland's (discussed above), Hunthausen's call to conversion necessitates a search for something new, in fact, "a new version of Church." Metaphorically, "version" suggests a particular form or point of view. In telling stories, one version may differ from another because of the vantage point used by each narrator. In this statement, when Hunthausen writes of "a new version of Church," he indicates that our vantage point stems from our conversion through faith and baptism. From this common vantage point, we are impelled to search out a new version of church that is whole and just.

In the four metaphors discussed above, the prevailing images include: returning to patterns of equality lived in the early church, submitting to radical change and reordering our household, stretching, letting go, and searching out a new way, and reaching toward a new version of church. The images are strong and uncompromising, if not original. The call to conversion can be ignored if one has heard the phrase too often, or if it is not preached with unction and urgency.

One of the more striking metaphors among those discussed is "household of faith." The term *household* is an important metaphor in the biblical tradition. Letty Russell delves into its uses, meanings, and eschatological sense in her book, *Household of Freedom*. She points out that it can evoke an oppressive image (e.g. one in which women and children are under the rule of a benevolent dictator) or an eschatological image (e.g. one in which women and children feel at home because no one there is locked into roles of domination and subordination). She notes that "a great deal of housecleaning is in order if the church is to live out its calling as an eschatological sign and instrument sign of God's household.[10]

The metaphors of reconciliation proclaim that there is a further task to be accomplished. Reconciliation is a restoration to union after a period of estrangement. It can also mean "making consistent" or "bringing to agreement." One statement, found in the Minnesota bishops' pastoral, calls women to a particular task of reconciliation in the context of unjust discrimination against them in the workplace, physical or sexual abuse, or of loss of public prestige or status because of their work in the home. The bishops say: "We encourage women working within the context of the teachings of the church and [their] Lord, to accept the challenge of righting the wrongs we have alluded to, and others besides." (19)

The metaphor of "righting the wrongs" suggests a process of reconciliation. In the above statement, it refers to specific injustices mentioned in the foregoing paragraphs and suggests that they can be turned around. *To right a wrong* is first to recognize an evil, then name it, then call

---

[10] Letty Russell, *Household of Freedom* (Philadelphia: Westminster Press, 1987), pp. 37 and 87.

others' attention to it, then strategize for ways which will correct it. *To right a wrong* means that obtaining the justice needed is a realizable goal with which to begin.

In the statement, the bishops urge women to accept the challenge of righting the wrongs done to them in society. By addressing them specifically, the bishops ask women to be the subjects of their own liberation. By naming the historical, contextual injustice of women's victimization and oppression and urging the oppressed to change that situation, the bishops speak from the position of liberation theology. They affirm that faith has a social dimension, that it urges us to build a society where the great "social dominations" will be no more.

Clark speaks specifically of the reconciliation needed between men and women and of Christ's part in that reconciliation. "Through prayer, reflection and genuine action inspired by new insights, our goal is to realize as church that profound reconciliation of men and women for which Christ hungers and of which he is the means." (22) While the metaphor, "for which Christ hungers," can be understood in a mystical sense, it can also be interpreted more concretely. To hunger is to crave, to be without essential sustenance. Clark's metaphor of Christ's being hungry for our reconciliation implies an urgency on our part to respond to his hunger.

Mahony ties an experience of reconciliation with the ongoing process of conversion in this metaphorical statement:

> Such a service [of reconciliation] could be a privileged moment here within our Archdiocese in the ongoing conversion to new ways of relating to one another as women and men in the Church, as members of the same family. (4)

By stating that a service of reconciliation could be a *privileged moment,* he implies that such a service might be a time of special grace not usually accessible in more common celebrations. He suggests that the service could move forward the conversion process necessary for "new ways of relating . . . as women and men in the Church." In addition, he aligns "men and women in the Church" with "members of the same family"—a juxtaposition that connotes equal belonging for both sexes.

In another statement, Mahony projects that the process of reconciliation "will require a painful dying to self for us all." The "dying" necessary in the spiritual life is familiar vocabulary to members of the church. Its usage here connects the experience with the dying, death, and resurrection of Christ and invites the recognition that each of us will experience a personal cost in achieving the unity desired.

A final metaphor picks up on a biblical theme and concludes our discussion on a note of hope. It comes from Weakland's task force report and is, fittingly, also the conclusion of that pastoral.

> Women *are* standing up straight. As this happens, some are indignant; many rejoice. We perceive this as the continuing challenge. It is our hope that the entire Church be energized by the search of women for wholeness and reconciliation. We believe that in this process, gender will shed its evil association with division and become what it was meant to be—a sacrament of unity, reconciliation, and wholeness. (12A)

For this extended metaphor, a gospel passage (Lk 13:10–17) is the context. In it, Jesus healed a stooped woman of an eighteen year old infirmity by laying his hand on her and saying, "Woman, you are free of your infirmity." The affirmation in the task force report that women *are* standing up straight today gives us a metaphor for the healing effect of liberation. When the authors state their hope that the entire church be "energized" by woman's search for wholeness and reconciliation, they suggest that a new vitality will be released. Finally, the authors state their faith that "in this process, gender will shed its evil association with division." Here, *gender* is personified; it will "shed its evil association with division"—like a snake shedding its skin in a mysterious process of renewal and transformation.

In the entire passage, metaphors of action and renewal dominate: the stooped stand up straight, women's search energizes the church, and gender sheds its evil associations. The metaphors suggest new life and wholeness. They engender hope because the visual images are life-giving and because the healing and liberation are not just for women but for the "entire church." It should be noted that these images are the result of extensive "listening sessions" and task force reflections on the question of women in the church. The ringing of a note of hope results from experience shared, not only goals wished for.

The metaphors of reconciliation bring out varying dimensions of the search for wholeness and unity. Those discussed above help us revision the way wrongs must be righted, imagine the hunger of Christ for the reconciliation of women and men, and sense the effect on the whole church of women's coming to wholeness. They suggest that conflicts have a public dimension and must be recognized and dealt with. Only then can the reconciliation women seek with society, with men, with themselves and their church, be actualized.

### *Conversion and Reconciliation: Conclusion*

While metaphors in the theme of conversion and reconciliation do not offer us new images of relationship, justice or church, they do address some processes which can serve to build new relationships. The metaphors reflect the struggle, such as the dying to self, needed to build a new church, particularly in relation to women's search for full and just participation in the mission of Christ. However, they fall short of calling for the concrete changes needed.

The bishops write about "letting go [of] stereotypes."

Can we hope that what will follow is a call for priests to "let go [of] clerical prerogatives" and share power for shaping the preaching, teaching, and social action with the people? In one pastoral sexism is designated as a "grievous sin." Can we hope that those who have remained silent until now will speak with outrage against the crimes that are perpetuated against women? The bishops call us to conversion, to return to early Christian ideals of true equality. Can we hope for a dismantling of clericalism so that ministry in the church can mean mutual empowerment? The bishops ask women to be the subjects of their own liberation. Can we hope that bishops will support those feminist base-communities which nurture liberated ways of relating and celebrating?

## Chapter 3

## Toward a New Vision of Church

The four gospels unequivocally attest to the presence of women at Jesus' tomb on Easter morning as the first witnesses of the resurrection (Mt 28:1–6; Mk 16:1–6; Lk 24:1–6; Jn 20:1). They are sent to proclaim the good news that the Lord had risen. Their call to discipleship is from Jesus himself, the one who was noted for his high regard for women. Throughout his life and before his ascension, Jesus refused to legitimate the myths about women promoted by the dominant culture and the educational tradition of his time. Later, as the early church grew rapidly, the churches of the Pauline mission had women as deacons, leaders, apostles, and prophets.[1]

Down through the ages, however, the old myths found an ever new place in the speeches, prayers, and books of his male followers. Only in recent times has another voice been heard in the church. At the Second Vatican Council, the bishops spoke to the Catholic community and to the world as follows:

> ... with respect to the fundamental rights of the person, every type of discrimination, whether social or cultural, whether based on sex, race, color, social condition, language, or religion, is to be overcome and eradicated as contrary to God's intent. For in truth it must still be regretted that fundamental personal rights are not yet being universally honored. Such is the case of a woman who is denied the right and freedom to choose a hus-

---

[1] Carolyn Osiek, RSCJ, "Women in the New Testament Church," in *Ministries,* Vol. 1, No. 4, April 1980, pp. 18–20. Osiek observes that radical egalitarianism often characterizes new religious movements in their early enthusiasm.

band, to embrace a state of life, or to acquire an education or cultural benefits equal to those recognized for men. (*Gaudium et Spes*, 29)

Since then, women have increasingly found new ways to participate in the faith life of the church and have left their mark on its educational institutions. In unprecedented numbers, women have obtained the degrees in scripture and theology which have given them access to the debates in the very forums which have legitimated their subjugation. Anne Patrick claims that this change accounts for the impact of the feminist movement on the church today.[2] The literature of Christian feminism not only has added new subject matter but has forced a critical reexamination of the premises and standards of existing scholarly work. Some people question whether Christianity can survive such a pervasive challenge to its self-understanding.[3] There are those who think that Christianity is irredeemably sexist and have left the church to find another forum to express their faith. There are others who have opted to stand within the tradition, "struggling to move beyond the critical task to a faithful revision of Christian theology."[4] Among the latter are women and men who are increasingly discouraged with the continuation of sexist attitudes, regulations, and structures.

Those who appreciate how quickly individual attitudes can change, especially as compared to the snail-like pace of social institutions, experience a sense of urgency concerning women's liberation in and for the church. Change not only comes about slowly; more often than not it arrives

---

[2] Anne E. Patrick, SNJM, "Toward Renewing 'The Life and Culture of Fallen Man': *Gaudium et Spes* as Catalyst for Catholic Feminist Theology," p. 56.

[3] Margaret Farley, RSM, "Can Faith Survive Injustice? A Question for Women in the Church" (unpublished paper, Washington, DC: NETWORK, 1984), p. 4.

[4] Farley, p. 4.

kicking and screaming. In the twenty-five years of conciliar renewal, the people of God have seen cataclysmic change—every level of faith life has been challenged to reach for a new maturity and relevance in this time of history. Women played a major part in this renewal, speaking for the right of responsible self-determination in such matters as birth control, and for the right to "embrace a state of life" to which many have felt called by God: the ministerial priesthood.

In earlier chapters we explored the institutional church's response to the women who raise such theological issues. Does the language of the U.S. bishops indicate they have internalized the new social reality? Does their language indicate their willingness to address the need of reforming tradition? A comparison may be made, between the church's view of women in the early part of this century and the view expressed in the pastoral letters of 1974–1987, which will help answer the first question. Then a further analysis of the metaphors, explored in the previous chapter, will lend itself to answering the second question.

## The Church's View of Women: Cardinal Gibbons to Pope Paul VI

An earlier chapter surveyed highlights of the U.S. hierarchy's teaching with regard to women as it related to critical events in U.S. history. Several key papal statements, related to women's search for equality and place in the home, were highlighted. Signs of a shift in viewpoint came into focus, beginning with Pope John XXIII's encyclical *Pacem in Terris*. The new view was seen to be further articulated in the documents of Vatican II which emphasized the equality of the sexes. Below, the key insights of Chapter I are recapitulated in order to draw out the likenesses and differences in the teachings of U.S. bishops in the period following Vatican Council II.

Cardinal Gibbons' admonitions about women's "place" in the early part of the twentieth century can be understood as a representative articulation of patriarchal thinking. It is characterized by a hierarchical viewpoint, one which sees male domination as natural and as required by the moral order. He asked, "Why should a woman lower herself to sordid politics?" a question which metaphorically announced the ideal view that women be "above" the "dirty" work of shaping culture and society. He insisted that "When a woman enters the political arena, she goes outside the sphere for which she was intended . . . she loses the exclusiveness, respect and dignity to which she is entitled in her home." Paradoxically, the cardinal reinforced the traditional idea of a separate and exalted role for women which effectively reduced them to the status of minors.

Metaphors in the above statements disclose dimensions of hierarchical thinking. The Cardinal admonishes woman not to "lower" herself, cautioning her against going "outside" the domestic sphere "for which she was intended." With protective paternalism, he reminds her that she will "lose" the respect and dignity to which she is "entitled" in her home. The spatial metaphors, and the references to entitlement and to the divine intent as to her proper sphere, all substantiate a view of reality that is unequivocally patriarchal. In sum, the metaphors serve to reinforce the appearance of timeless permanence in the structure of gender relations wherein men set policies about women.

The words of Pius XI and Pius XII continue the same themes in their encyclicals. They denounce women's efforts for equality and in very strong language remind them of their subordination to men. Women are to be the "heart" of the home, husbands "the head." Women are warned against a "proud autonomy" and reminded that "every woman is called to be a mother." The metaphors here disclose an epistemological view similar to that of Cardinal Gibbons. In this view, knowledge of reality is a male prerogative which gives the knower the power to name and to control.[5] In the church, this incomplete understanding of what knowledge is expresses itself in a hierarchical structure: men maintain the top positions of governance; women assume the subordinate roles, upholding the emotional and moral life of the human community. The remarks of the popes reveal their own operative insights into a rapidly advancing technological society in many parts of the world, a rise in women's participation in the work force because of the world war, and a steadily increasing consciousness of equality with men that was strengthening women's political will for change.

With the teaching of John XXIII the dual consciousness characteristic of patriarchal mentality continues to be represented, but some change in official church viewpoint is evident. Recognizing that women are in the work force to stay, the pope takes a new tack. "Women have the right to working conditions in accordance with their requirements and their duties as wives and mothers." (*Pacem in Terris* 19) The ambiguity expressed in this statement is representative of a viewpoint that is informed not only by traditional theology and the teachings of the papacy earlier in this century but also contemporary realities. Thus, women have "the right" to decent working conditions, but their "special" role is also underscored as "wives and mothers." In the same encyclical, John XXIII affirms women's growing consciousness of their human dignity and consequent rejection of debasing treatment. That year, 1963, marked the first time in this century that official church teaching addressed women with this insight. It coincided with the opening of Vatican Council II, which was destined to unfold

---

[5] See Bernard J.F. Lonergan in *Insight: A Study of Human Understanding*, for an explanation of cognitional theory, an exploration of the subject as knower. See also his book, *Method in Theology* (Minneapolis: The Seabury Press, 1979), pp. 213–214, especially 238–239.

more fully the themes of equality and human dignity, signifying the beginning of what may be seen as a paradigm shift in consciousness about the role of women in society.

In the period of renewal after the council, the fertile imagination of the whole church gave birth to abundant life. Women, especially those in democratic nations, began to explore the possibilities for their enhanced role in the church; feminist scholarship uncovered the extent of male bias which had dominated theology and church teaching for centuries; and church leaders were hard put to meet the ensuing challenges and developments of women's participation in the mission of the church. During the reign of Paul VI, the Vatican issued a surfeit of statements, documents, and commission reports on the role of women in society and the church. The characteristic theme in this literature is the preoccupation with woman's "nature" as distinct and therefore her "place" as being different.

Several points can be made in regard to the material referred to above. First, the view of reality as expressed in the teaching of the magisterium and the official church in the U.S. is corollary to the social form of patriarchy that has dominated western civilization for more than two thousand years. Patriarchy is a hierarchical way of organizing social relations, a form that establishes men in a shared relationship of dominance over women. This social form affects our conceptually organized knowledge, consequently providing women and men with different vantage points as well as an understanding of power relations.

Legitimating symbols are necessary to all forms of governance. A patriarch often sees himself as protector of the family, responsible and caring for those under his rule. Those subject to his power are of necessity dependent. In a patriarchal society, the myth of spiritual femininity does not function as a symbol of woman's capacity for leadership or equality with men. Instead, as Madonna Kolbenschlag points out, it is "invoked as a justification for her 'natural' role as mother, support person, chief cheerleader in a sphere set apart from 'real' life and the affairs of men."[6] The myths of man's superiority and woman's "natural" lower status have fostered the dual consciousness prevalent in male dominated societies.

Thus, Cardinal Gibbon's words and those of Pius XI and Pius XII may be read as a characteristic manifestation of the general social condition that has until now played out among women and men in a variety of forms and places. Their words are instructive for this study, in that they disclose the power relations in the church, within which men's lives and interests have circumscribed those of women. Their words reflect what Bernard Lonergan calls a distortion—a group bias, which continues to reinforce the positions of those who hold the bias. This bias infects the understanding, judging, and decisions not only of those who hold it but of those who are affected by it.[7]

Second, it is evident from the study of ecclesial writings that church officials perceive woman's "nature" to be something special and different from that of man, whose nature is seen as normative. It is not women who define their "nature" as different. It is men who desire to structure gender solidarity and who have so defined women's "nature" that their appropriateness for serving in auxiliary roles, in society and in the church, seems self-evident. In addition, women's "rights" are designated by men as those compatible with their supposedly distinctive "nature," definitively established in the divine order of creation. Ultimately, the appeal is to an authoritative interpretation of the creation story in Genesis. The point must

---

[6] Madonna Kolbenschlag, HM, "Women and the Church: Misbegotten Myths" (unpublished paper), p. 7.

[7] Lonergan, *Insight*, pp. 222–225. He explains that "the bias of development involves a distortion. The advantage of one group commonly is disadvantageous to another, and so some part of the energies of all groups is diverted to the supererogatory of devising and implementing offensive and defensive mechanisms" (p. 224).

be made, however, that biblical materials are themselves products of acculturation. Raymond Brown points out the task of biblical interpretation to take into account that process of acculturation:

> Since the Bible contains the word of God in the words of men, these texts reflect the sociology of God's people respectively in the first century A.D. and the eleventh century B.C. They cannot be repeated as normative today in a different sociology without first investigating whether the change of social condition does not require a different expression of God's will for his people.[8]

Thus, official church pronouncements on women should be made in conjunction with the insights of contemporary biblical scholarship, in addition to the data available from the social sciences.[9]

Third, in the literature discussed above, it is clear that the idealization of women goes hand in hand with their subordination. By singling out "ideal" qualities or emphasizing the nurturing role many women have had in family life and attributing these to the "nature" of woman, the church aims at a moral regulation of women based on the

---

[8] Raymond Brown, *Biblical Reflections on Crises Facing the Church* (New York: Paulist Press, 1975), p. 51.

[9] I would hope to find references to current feminist scholarship in future pastoral letters/publications from the U.S. hierarchy. Ancient categories for understanding "woman" need to be put aside, and benchmark scholarship in women's studies must be taken seriously. For example, see Phyllis Trible, *God and the Rhetoric of Sexuality* (Philadelphia: Fortress Press, 1978), pp. 72–143, for a rhetorical critical analysis of the creation story. Other scholars whose works reorder our culturally-conditioned thinking include Jean Baker Miller, *Toward a New Psychology of Women* (Boston: Beacon Press, 1976) and Carol Gilligan, *In a*

## Toward a New Vision of Church 107

limitation of what men consider appropriate forms of thought, expression, and behavior for the female sex. Women are at once idealized and politically disempowered. In addition, the predominant and emphatic use of generic (male) terms and of masculine imagery for God serves to confirm this form of gender subordination, which renders women passive, silent, and, finally, often invisible.

In contrast to the language used to express what was deemed appropriate for women in a previous era, the language of the U.S. bishops in recent times reflects their recognition that women have attained a more adult status in the church. The language of churchmen has undergone notable change. Although they are at times identified as the problem, women are not rebuked or silenced. The language of resistance has given way to the language of recognition that women are creative and responsible beings, capable of initiating life in the church and in society.

Characteristically, the metaphors in the pastoral letters on women reflect an often probing analysis of the traditions in the church and society which have kept women passive and marginal. For example, there is recognition of "a new age for women," of how much "the church needs the Christian woman in an ecclesial role," of the need to work for the time "when full partnership will be a reality," of the necessity for reforming "attitudes and practices among us which fall short of recognizing the full dignity and stature of every person."

A survey of the one hundred and fifty metaphors compiled for this study reveals that there are U.S. bishops who

---

*Different Voice* (Cambridge: Harvard University Press, 1982). Miller explains how women as victims and subordinates have denied their anger and become highly attuned to the responses of the dominators, acting as the quintessential mediators, adaptors, and soothers. Gilligan's work on the female construction of reality and moral development shows how women's experience, as a relational bias, needs to be integrated into developmental psychology.

are grappling with the issues of feminism and their implications for the church. It would follow that the bishops' recognition of woman's equal dignity and responsibility with man would necessarily lead to their desire to change those structures which continue to maintain women's inferior status. Further analysis of the metaphors will suggest the extent to which the bishops critique the existing structures in the church. To the extent that the bishops recognize that these basic structures, and not women, are the fundamental problem, they give us intimations of a future church which will call women to a full expression of their personhood and moral and social responsibility as equal partners with men.

## The Church's View of Women Today

The previous chapter unpacked metaphors in the twelve pastoral letters to see what they reflect about the basic epistemologies of the writers. The metaphors were explored as filters which invite us to see the domain of awareness from which they arose. Their content suggests yet another organization, for they reveal distinct ways in which the bishops perceive and react to apparent paradox. It is proposed here that the metaphors contribute to three different levels of the ongoing discussion about the role of women in today's church, depending on the extent to which they intimate a critical analysis of the existing system. While some metaphors reflect a position that a full expression of woman's personhood and gift for ministry can be accommodated within the present church structures, others bring a critical analysis to the existing system, or paradigm. By introducing such a critique, the writers imply that the problem is not women but the structures. Those bishops intimate that nothing less than a revolution is necessary to appropriate the paradigm of true equality which Jesus introduced and which the developed human consciousness of our day demands.

The three different levels of discussion correspond with

Thomas Kuhn's theory of paradigm shift. Kuhn examines the sociological sense of a paradigm, which, he says, "stands for the entire constellation of beliefs, values, techniques, and so on shared by the members of a given community."[10] He discusses the invention of new theories and indicates that there are, in principle, only three types of phenomena about which a new theory might be developed. (Theory, in this context, connotes a structure limited in scope and nature.) The first type of phenomena are already well explained by the existing paradigm, and these seldom provide either motive or point of departure for theory construction.

A second class of phenomena consists of those whose nature is indicated by existing paradigms but whose details can be understood only through further theory articulation. The third type of phenomena are the recognized anomalies whose characteristic feature is their stubborn refusal to be assimilated to existing paradigms. Kuhn shows that this type alone gives rise to new theories. Using Kuhn's framework, we can discover which metaphors contribute to the three levels of discussion about the role of women in the church.

## *The First Level: "Prisoners of a Culture"*

On one level of discussion, the institutional church may be heard to offer women a framework for fuller participation within the existing structures. At this level, the discussion may be recognized as a reinstatement of the "old vision" with an encouragement to women to do more and better what women have already been allowed to do. The metaphors function to maintain the existing social order, and no change in church structures is contemplated. The discussion of women's role in the church is characterized by justification of things as they are, and sometimes it even

---

[10] Thomas Kuhn, *The Structure of Scientific Revolutions* (Chicago: University of Chicago Press, 1962, 1970), p. 175. I am indebted to Catherine Lacey, RSCJ, for introducing me to Kuhn's theory and suggesting its applicability in this study.

includes an appeal to the authority of tradition and of official church teaching.

Metaphors which contribute to the discussion at the first level are found in each of the topic categories explored. The understanding that men and women are "prisoners of a culture" (Borders: 5) and that "society's pattern for women is pre-set" (Minnesota bishops: 8) serves to reinforce the sense of permanence of cultural stereotypes and justifies their existence. The reference to the "newer marks that are strangely feminine: welcome, friendship, love, hospitality, warmth . . . (Dozier: 5), which affect our experience at the local church, indicates a recognition that change is occurring for the good within existing structures of the church. Another metaphorical expression, "the universal woman is one of the great and credible transmitters of the gospel" (Dozier: 4), has the ring of encouraging women to fuller participation, but signals no need for change in the structures which block them. Dozier's pattern of universalizing "woman" also serves to render invisible the concrete experience and contribution of *each* woman, which is more unique than common.

It is important to note that the principle of complementarity as expressed in metaphor seems to arise from and contribute to this level of discussion. There are several reasons for this. First, there is an appeal to the authority of a traditional theological interpretation of the first two chapters of Genesis. The mode of reference might be as pithy as: "In the divine design, men and women are meant to complement each other." (Maher: 7) Second, to invoke this principle is to justify those theories about the "nature" of woman which render her participation subordinate. Third, this principle arises from a theory about male/female relationships that is integrally connected with the existing hierarchical structure and related to the social process of gender relationships.[11] In sum, the notion of

---

[11] See Joan W. Scott, "Gender: A Useful Category of Analysis," in the *American Historical Review* 9 (1986), especially pp.

complementarity cannot be seen as a point of departure for a theory construction compatible with an understanding of a single anthropology, recognized as "the sounder basis for theological discussion."[12] Neither is it compatible with a transformative model of person which points to the element of radical human freedom in determining what human nature will become.

Those metaphors which contribute to this first level of discussion may be said to have emerged from within a particular historical context of the institutional church, noted for its strong resistance to change. Traditional assumptions about society and the church are maintained as the

---

1067–1069. In her two-part definition, Scott says that gender not only is a constitutive element of social relationships based on perceived differences between the sexes, but is also a primary way of signifying relationships of power. "Changes in the organization of social relationships," she says, "always correspond to changes in representations of power . . ." (p. 1067). A recent example of this principle appears in a statement by Cardinal Eduardo Pironio. Looking to the 1987 World Synod of Bishops on the laity, he said that women's role in the church should be discussed—but not as a "feminist-style revindication of women's rights. . . ." "At issue is not the desire to totally put oneself on the same level as men," he said, "but a recognition of the complementariness of women in the evangelizing mission of the church, as holy Mary had in the redeeming work of Jesus." *National Catholic Reporter*, Vol. 23: No. 23, April 3, 1987, p. 3.

[12] This is the conclusion reached in a *1978 Research Report* of the Catholic Theological Society of America. Quoted in Anne Carr, "Theological Anthropology and the Experience of Women," *Chicago Studies* (Vol. 19: No. 2, Summer 1980), p. 121. Carr points out that it is a dual anthropology, affirmed often in church documents, that "emphasizes the unchanging structures of nature and view revelation, tradition, theology and ethics as past-oriented: what is has been given and *must not be changed. New knowledge of the human person, derived from the human sciences, is irrelevant to theological discussion since its goal is to preserve the past order as natural, as the order of creation, as revealed*" (p. 121—emphasis added).

writers approach this topic with metaphors that reinforce the rules of social relationships. There are, however, significantly fewer metaphors in this category than in the following two.

## *The Second Level: "New Models of Participation"*

At a second level, some metaphors help us to identify what the perceived problem is, and what action steps might be taken in order to correct it. The problem is identified as women themselves, with their evolved consciousness and demand for equal treatment with men in the church. The level of discussion here is characterized by problem solving. However, solutions are sought within the existing structures and build on the principle of women's unique "nature."

At this second level, there are metaphors which indicate that the bishops recognize something new in woman's consciousness, a newness which presents a problem within the church. Sometimes they offer ways to accommodate it. However, in these metaphors, the "problem" is identified as "woman" or woman's awakening, not the existing church structures. Dozier's effort to describe women's new consciousness results in three metaphors in this category. He says that women are "a live issue today in the international consciousness" (1) and "woman's awakening is indeed as global as inflation." (3) He writes that "For the woman, the narrow institutions of the past seem more dispensable than ever, because woman has discovered her sister. Their mutual embrace reaches around the world; it is feminist, reverential, even ecclesial." (3) This trio of metaphorical expressions seeks to disrupt the readers' epistemic world so that previous understandings have to be revised. By drawing the reader into paradox, the bishop invites a new perception of a complex world where rigid categories no longer hold. The metaphors indicate that Dozier was extraordinarily conscious of the impact of the women's movement on society as well as the church and desirous of communicating his insight. However, he

## Toward a New Vision of Church

did not connect the impact with the need for social reconstruction.

Other metaphors which contribute to the second level of discussion show a concern for problem-solving. The statement "Equality needs to be nourished by new models of participation" (Minnesota bishops: 12) suggests that the principle of equality needs to be strengthened. It further implies that "new models" can be accommodated within the present structure of church. No hint of changing it occurs. Similarly, the assertion that "In our time the church clearly desires that women should become aware of the greatness of their mission and take their equal, if sometimes different place alongside their brothers in Christ" (Gerety: 11) reflects a grasp of women's desire for equality, but it seems to arise from the hope of accommodating women in the existing system, not from a desire to change this system. Mahony's phrase, "We need to recover a greater sense of men and women working collaboratively, side by side" (3), offers a variation on this theme. His metaphor suggests there was a previous relationship of collaboration and offers a similar "side by side" image of the sexes working together in the future.

There is also the metaphor of "the further matter which inevitably enters any discussion on the role of women. . . ." (Borders: 10) The "further matter" (that of ordaining women to the priesthood) could be interpreted as a question to be solved in some future time, or in terms of a further challenge which is outside present church discipline. Both interpretations hint at the possibility of change; both also keep a respectful distance from the question.

The metaphor "partners in the mission of Christ" (Gerety: 9), like that of "partners in the task of working to bring about the Kingdom of justice and peace . . ." (Mahony: 2), can be read several ways, depending on the interpretation of equality in partnership. It may refer to an eschatological future when women and men are fully redeemed in Christ. It may refer to a notion of equal partnership that is in accord with a perception of women's different "nature." Or it may mean equal partners in the sense of vocational call and opportunity to serve. The first two interpretations would align the metaphor with the discussion at level two. The last interpretation would indicate a third stage of discussion.

Many of the metaphors at the second level of discussion focus on short term rather than long term outcomes. They reveal that some traditional assumptions about what can and cannot be changed are in place. The metaphors help us understand several ways that some bishops are attempting to make sense of the feminist challenge to the church: the new consciousness women have gained is pervasive and must be helped to impact the church positively; the working relationships of men and women need improvement; and the major question of ordaining women cannot be solved at this time.

### *The Third Level: "A New Version of Church"*

There is a decided shift from second level discussion to third level analysis. Only at the third level is there revealed a comprehension of the depth of the problem and the needed critique of the dominant paradigm and corresponding worldview. The shift from identifying *women* as the problem to *analysis of the system* indicates an awareness that a new theory or paradigm is needed, because the challenges to the current paradigm cannot be accommodated within its system. The problem is identified as the paradigm or system itself, not the challenges which necessitate a change. In metaphorical terms, the new wine cannot be contained in old wineskins. Or, as Rosemary Radford Ruether puts it, "Women don't want a piece of the pie; they want to change the whole recipe."[13]

Metaphors which hint at a critique of the structures of the church are found in each of the topic categories. Some

---

[13] I am indebted to Cora Twohig-Moengangongo for suggesting this metaphor, cited in a class by Professor Ellen Leonard at the Toronto School of Theology, January 1985.

metaphors direct our thoughts to the early church for a model, such as in the statement that "women's role in the church today is of supreme importance for the rediscovery by believers of the true face of the church." (Gerety: 11) This is an example of a "generative" metaphor, one which acts like a "springboard"[14] for transition to a new, more complex understanding of church. It directs attention to the faithful ("believers") who must be about the search for the "true face of the church." The contextual meaning of the search is what is new—"women's role in the church today." The metaphor is not an evaluative or judgmental statement; it simply cues a descriptive inquiry into the faith community. It also gives status and recognition to "women's role" as it relates to the authenticity of the church.

Several metaphors indicate more directly that there is a need for analysis, for a critique of the existing paradigm. For example, the statement "Neither society nor church can any longer tolerate the imposition of barriers in women's paths of growth" (Minnesota bishops: 6) contains a metaphor which not only suggests a need for system analysis but also implies a willingness to change that system which perpetuates injustice. In another metaphor, there is recognition of the unjust structures and their effect on women, and, further, a reference to the caste system of the all-male priesthood. "Let us understand with compassion the legitimate anger on the part of some women toward those structures or traditions which have demanded and expected less than full priesthood from them." (Gerety: 2) This metaphorical statement does not camouflage powerful feelings. Rather, it suggests that women's anger has been listened to and understood, and points to the existing

---

[14] Suresh Srivastva and Frank J. Barrett, "The Transforming Nature of Metaphors in Group Development: A Study in Group Theory," in *Human Relations*, Vol. 41: No. 1, 1988, pp. 50–54. The theorists propose that "generative metaphors" frame socially constructed reality in a new, more complex way.

paradigm as the cause of the anger.[15] It is not clear, however, which "priesthood" is intended here. Is it the priesthood of the offering community, which is the priesthood belonging to all the baptized, or the ministerial priesthood, which requires ordination?

Some metaphorical statements go further still, calling explicitly for fundamental conversion and hinting at the social reconstruction necessary to achieve justice. "We continue to look critically at existing structures, to discern whether they foster or hinder full personhood of women and men in the Church." (Hunthausen: 4) Here, the relationship between structures and potentiality is recognized, as well as a commitment to examine "existing structures" with a view to changing them. Initial steps we can make toward the changes are suggested through another metaphor. "We are being asked to stretch our horizons a bit. We are being asked to let go of stereotypes. We are being asked to search out what following Christ together as men and women really means." (Weakland: 1) Our attitudes, our worldview, need to be converted. The problem is identified as the system itself, not women. The existing structures in the church are recognized as inimical to the full and just participation of women in Christ's mission, so there is insight that a new version of church must be sought. It is people and attitudes that will foster new insights and theories which will change the system. Offering concrete suggestions to achieve this change, one bishop writes that "women must increasingly be placed in policy formation and decision-making levels within the church." (Mahony: 3)

Other metaphors hint at this new version of church.

---

[15] In Gerety's archdiocese, concrete action was recommended to address the issues which caused the anger. When the senate of priests set up a task force to study the pastoral and make recommendations on the basis of it, eight strong and far-reaching recommendations were made, four of which called for development of the relationship between women and men in ministry.

"We must work together to reverse this trend [of racism and sexism within the church] and return to the early Christian ideal of true equality among all persons." (Buswell: 2) In this statement, we are reminded of the early days of the church before the accommodation of Christianity to patriarchy. "The early Christian ideal" which comes to mind is spelled out in the Acts of the Apostles and in some of the epistles, a vision that is freshly articulated from the disciples' personal experience of Christ's presence and preaching.

The relationship of the present-day church with Christ is articulated in still other metaphors, among them: "As we preach Christ to the world, we must undergo conversion and put our own household of faith in order." (Gerety: 2) This is a familiar exhortation—to practice within the church what we preach in the world. For some, the inference of disorder in the household of faith could imply a need for more stringent control from those in authority. But since the metaphor is coupled with a call to conversion, it can be better interpreted to mean a *new* ordering, based on a true equality of persons. A critique of the dominant paradigm is indicated, not problem-solving.

Such metaphors which contribute to the third level of discussion are similar to the class of phenomena which Kuhn says is encountered when attempts at further articulation of the existing paradigm fail. The failure results because the anomaly, in this case the necessity of incorporating women in the life of the church at all levels, stubbornly refuses to be assimilated to the existing paradigm.[16] How, then, does needed change occur? Kuhn says that *the conversion process lies at the heart of the revolutionary process.*[17] The metaphors in this study which call for conversion and a critique of the system come from another horizon than those which maintain traditional representations of experience.

---

[16] Kuhn, *The Structure of Scientific Revolutions*, pp. 97–98.
[17] Kuhn, p. 204.

More significant than any particular new concepts may be the tendency of thought as expressed in the metaphors, its gradient and its direction. Whereas Dozier wrote predominantly of women's new consciousness, Mahony, more than twelve years later, could write that women must be included in the church's policy-making and decision-making levels. Because a study of metaphors is a study of the way thought moves, it suggests the possibility of still newer concepts that may open up greater understanding. To unpack the metaphors related to women's role in the church is to see not only how far the bishops have come in the development of their understandings but also to imagine how far they can be expected to go in the future.

## Imagining the Future

If we understand the metaphors studied here to be multi-vocal, with many meanings linked to a core meaning which takes on a "steering function"[18] for future action and future perceptions, we can begin to imagine a "new version of church." What might the church look like when it calls women to a full expression of their personhood, their moral and social responsibility?

In imagining the future church, we can build on the promise of Galatians 3:28 that there is neither Jew nor Greek, slave nor free, male nor female, but that all are one in Christ Jesus. This describes a church that is liberated from the worldview of patriarchy. Shared policy-making and decision-making will be the norm. The structure will be collegial, mutually inclusive of women and men, who together will address the ongoing concerns of the faith community, from human sexuality and family life to the exercise of leadership and the moral dimension of contemporary issues. These areas of concern will have been aired

---

[18] Suresh Srivastva and Frank J. Barrett, "The Transforming Nature of Metaphors in Group Development," p. 47.

## Toward a New Vision of Church

openly wherever there are communities of faith and struggle.

Patterns of domination and subordination will have given way to mutuality and trust, which is the basis for mature love. Mutuality in relationship—like the relationship of *koinonia*[19] in the New Testament—will empower us as church to reach out to the poor and those in crisis as well as attend to the global and the cosmic. In a church where true mutuality is the basis of relationships, we will recognize one another's autonomy; allowance of opposition and conflict will attest to its authenticity.[20] Communities daring to share power will gradually change the value system in the church, where there will be opportunities for full participation regardless of sex, race, or marital status. Authority will function as empowerment for service, in the style of Jesus.

One result of sharing our feelings, experiences, and reflections will be a revolutionary approach to God. It will challenge the ancient concept of God as father, as male, and as a being always portrayed as one sex to the total exclusion of the other sex. The collective consciousness of the faithful will reflect a fuller revelation of God. God the omnipotent one will be revealed once again as powerless, like a woman in labor, Isaiah tells us. God mighty in battle will be revealed once again as the defender of widows and orphans, the God of peace. Recognizing that tradition itself is limited, the faithful will look to their own ongoing experience as a people of God for further revelation of the Holy Spirit, ever stirring us on to an ever new understanding of what it is to be human, to be in the image of God. That Spirit will give us the

---

[19] *Koinonia* assumes a common bond in Jesus Christ that establishes mutual community (see 1 Cor 10:16–17).

[20] See Rosemary Radford Ruether, *Sexism and God-Talk* (Boston: Beacon Press, 1983), especially the section "Ministry as Mutual Empowerment," pp. 206–210. See also Elisabeth Moltmann-Wendell, *A Land Flowing with Milk and Honey*, p. 139.

passion and energy necessary to struggle for change and to build the community of God on earth.

## Conclusion

Some final questions remain. What does this body of literature mean for the church in the U.S. today? We take the bishops seriously and listen to their teaching as a possible mediation of God's word for us. They have pondered the church's teaching on human dignity, which provides the context for their teaching on human rights. They have investigated the question of culture and, specifically, they have begun to take seriously some feminist issues dominant in the American culture. We have seen through metaphor how some bishops interpret women's situation, with a curious combination of old formulations and new insights. These are at times stubbornly anachronistic and, at other times, progressive.

These bishops are trying to stand with women coming to full personhood, by applying gospel principles in critiquing the culture in which women's self-understanding and ways of knowing are formed. They have recalled themes of the tradition and reinterpreted them for our time. They have encouraged women to do whatever genuinely worthwhile things they can do in public life, to participate in the fullest possible range of activities. But, as Margaret Brennan points out, if the bishops are to deal with the reality that women have no political voice in the church and if they are to probe the real causes of women's oppression, "they will be led inevitably to confront the pervasiveness of patriarchy of which they themselves are the official carriers. If and when this happens, we may well see a pastoral that deals with the call to a conversion from sexist and androcentric ideologies that find expression in moral, ministerial, and theological prescriptions."[21]

---

[21] Margaret Brennan, IHM, "The Pastoral on Women: What Should the Bishops Say?" in *America*, Vol. 152: No. 19 (May 18, 1985), p. 411.

The most hopeful sign for the church in the pastorals studied here is in the call to conversion and, with it, the challenge to "critically examine" the structures of the church. In this there is the possibility that men in the church will seek to understand the experience of women, will listen to them, and will come to recognize that the present structures are inimical to women's growth to full human personhood. Chapter I described how the papal commission on birth control underwent a change of heart and mind when its members listened to the testimony of women. It was evident, however, that the magisterium chose to draw its own conclusion and uphold the authority of previous popes in its teaching on birth control.

In preparing pastoral letters for the church in the U.S., the bishops have invited the people of God to participate in a dialogical and processive process. This is a "new method of episcopal teaching" according to Richard McCormick, one which "reflects much more a concentric model of the Church than a pyramidal one."[22] It involves not only the consultation of scholars and experts in a given field, but also listening to the experience of those who are directly affected by the teaching. A similar process was used to some extent in the development of many of the pastorals studied in this book, most notably in the archdiocese of Milwaukee. The so-called "listening process" developed there became a model for the listening sessions that U.S. bishops held throughout the United States in preparation for their NCCC pastoral letter addressing the concerns of women. In such a process, real listening changes the listener; when these changes are in conflict with a tradition, a new level of dialogue must occur.

This kind of listening which must continue between the bishops and women is what could lead to a pastoral

---

[22] Richard McCormick, S. J., "Bishops as Teachers and Jesuits as Listeners" in *Studies in the Spirituality of Jesuits*, Vol. 18: No. 3 (May, 1986), p. 3.

letter of import.[23] When the bishops and women commit themselves to "stay at the table" until real dialogue has occurred, something altogether new and creative will happen in the church. The commitment of time and thought, and the necessity of a heart willing to be converted, may appear to be beyond the realm of what is reasonable, much less possible, but such a dialogue is foundational to finding "the true face of the church." Commissioning a woman to write a pastoral, even if it must "pass" the committee working with her, will not ensure the kind of meeting of hearts and minds that must occur if we are to be faithful followers of Jesus.

The twelve pastoral letters which preceded "Partners in Redemption" have an historical value and may perhaps carry the seeds of the church of the future. Have the bishops offered us any new imagery or language in their metaphors which help us envision the more authentic "face of the church"? Many of the metaphors arise out of incomplete epistemological premises which cannot help us image a new era. Other metaphors contribute to a process epistemology and may help us change the way we think about something. We have seen that some bishops, notably Dozier, Gerety, Maher, and Clark, have employed a metaphoric process which helps new knowledge come into existence. Metaphors proceed from images that give rise to

---

[23] See Mary Hunt, "Limited Partners," in *Waterwheel*, Vol. 1: No. 2 (Summer, 1988). Hunt proposes that bishops and women model partnership in writing together a pastoral letter. She says, "We will surely be asked, 'What do Catholic women want?' The answer is justice. We want a fifty-fifty deal, assets and liabilities alike. We do not want the counter-cultural approach of the church which protects women without the equally counter-cultural approach of the church which has women name our own reality. We do not want the largess of the bishops for a few women deacons who will solve their priest shortage by their boundless energy and ministerial skill, unless the episcopacy is open to women" (p. 3).

understanding. These images are grounded in experience. The experience of women opens up a broader horizon of knowledge than has been represented in the church. Because the metaphors in the pastorals are more representative of a search than a discovered truth, they suggest that we are still at the beginning stage of the major paradigm shift which calls into question all previous knowing that has excluded women.

The energizing speech of metaphor can be instrumental in birthing the new paradigm. We need their power to reimagine the world with a new language that recognizes the full humanity of women and men. Gerhart and Russell as students of metaphor theorize that "it is the ontological flash that creates the sense of presence before that which is. . . . An ontological flash is an event which creates conviction. Such an event explodes conceptual horizons. . . . These moments of insight . . . instill a sense of completion, of perfection, and of beauty that prevents question."[24] There is no further question about women and their rightful participation in a world of being. There is unceasing question about how that knowing is lived out in a church that is faithful to this new understanding.

I conclude that rational analysis alone will not bring change. We need symbols, images, metaphors of who we are in this period of change, metaphors to help us choose what the human future will be. The imaginative use of language and insight will help us picture what God has in mind for the church tomorrow, and what our part is to be in the process. When the church welcomes women as equal partners in the mission of Christ, that welcome will reflect that a major shift is occurring in the way men and women see reality. Today, because women have been marginal in church structures and without political voice, women's

---

[24] Mary Gerhart and Allan Russell, *Metaphoric Process: The Creation of Scientific and Religious Understanding* (Fort Worth: Texas Christian University Press, 1984), p. 151.

cultural wisdom has not been brought to bear sufficiently within the life of the church. We can hope in the future that metaphors, which begin with experience, will image a whole new range of what it is to be human and what it is to be church.

# *Afterword*

Shortly after the U.S. Roman Catholic bishops (NCCB) decided to write a pastoral letter addressing women's concerns, they consulted hundreds of U.S. women and men who bring different perspectives to the issues. It is now more than two years since the first draft was circulated and drew response, and six months since the second draft was made public and stirred strong reactions. The LCWR and other national groups have urged the bishops to withdraw the draft and vote against its publication at their November 1990 meeting. Instead, they say, begin implementation of the recommended initiatives given in the conclusion of the pastoral. These include: denouncing physical, sexual, economic and psychological acts of injustice against women; working to improve wage-setting procedures, starting with church institutions; advocating the use of flex-time and job sharing, along with the guarantee of comparable pay for comparable work; and responding with imagination and courage to eradicate the injustice that keeps us from the full stature of Christ.

Most recently, the Vatican has suggested that consultation with bishops' conferences of other countries on this pastoral letter would be appropriate. In September 1990, the NCCB Administrative Committee decided to defer a vote on the pastoral, pending the worldwide consultation which Rome has recommended. This decision may bode well; it all depends on how the process of consultation is orchestrated. At the 1988 Synod on the Laity, both the pope and representatives from church conferences around the world acknowledged the need everywhere to recognize the role of women in the church today. This perception grew as the sessions of the synod progressed. If the desired consultation on the pastoral asks church hierarchy to dialogue with women who name their own reality, we could see a new moment in the struggle for equality.

The consultation could take the form of an educative process, which would encourage the needed ongoing conversion. If the process includes those in the autonomous, self-determining women's movements unfolding in the different civilizations of the world, the church could find itself the point of coalescence of movements for change. If the process includes women everywhere who minister the gospel in ways that Rome has not yet imagined, the church will find that a new epoch has already begun.

Together, the people of God could envision new ways, find new words, create new possibilities to transform the existing social order, and discern a greater human potential. Gradually, the further self-revelation of our non-sexist God will prompt us to rediscover the vision of church Jesus died for and to become his community of equal disciples.

October 1990

## Exhibit A. Bishops' Pastoral Letters 1974–1987

| (Arch*) Bishop | (Arch*) Diocese | Year | Title |
|---|---|---|---|
| Leo T. Maher | San Diego | August 1974 | Women in the New World |
| Carrol T. Dozier | Memphis | January 1975 | Woman: Intrepid and Loving |
| Charles A. Buswell | Pueblo | December 1975 | Ecclesial Affirmative Action: A Matter of Simple Justice |
| William D. Borders* | Baltimore* | August 1977 | Woman in the Church: Reflections on Women in the Mission and Ministry of the Church |
| Minnesota Bishops | Minnesota | March 1979 | Woman: Pastoral Reflections |
| Raymond G. Hunthausen* | Seattle* | April 1980 | Pastoral Statement on Women |
| Peter L. Gerety* | Newark* | February 1981 | Women in the Church |
| John S. Cummins | Oakland | October 1981 | Women in Ministry |
| Victor H. Balke / Raymond A. Lucker | Crookston / New Ulm | October 1981 | Male and Female God Created Them |
| Matthew H. Clark | Rochester | April 1982 | The Fire in the Thornbush |
| Rembert G. Weakland, OSB* | Milwaukee* | November 1982 | Task Force Report on the Role of Women in the Church of Southeast Wisconsin |
| Roger Mahony* | Los Angeles* | August 1987 | Just as the Women Said |

# Exhibit B. Responses of Eleven Bishops to the Survey

1. Frequent responses to the question: Was the pastoral letter written to meet a specific need in the diocese? Did it address any "burning issues" in your diocese?

| **Percent of respondents** | **Response** |
|---|---|
| 18% | −No |
| 18% | −Written to address the role/position of women in the church |
| 18% | −address issues concerning women in ministry |
| 18% | −addresses the role of women in the local church of the archdiocese |
| 18% | −addresses women's fuller participation in the life of the church |

(To this question, responses fell into more than one category.)

2. Frequent responses to the question: Was the letter written at the suggestion of "grass roots" Catholics or out of your own inspiration?

| **Percent of respondents** | **Response*** |
|---|---|
| 73% | −both personal inspiration and others' suggestions (e.g. grass roots Catholics, a group |

|     |                          |
| --- | ------------------------ |
|     | or committee) played a role |
| 27% | –primarily, own inspiration |

3. Frequent responses to the question: Was the letter part of a process?

| **Percent of respondents** | **Response** |
| --- | --- |
| 45% | –a committee/group collected information by means of a formal process (e.g. hearings, surveys, reports) |
| 36% | –a group of women provided material and/or consultation and dialogue |
| 18% | –there was minimal or no formal process |

4. Frequent responses to the question: What happened as a result of the pastoral letter?

| **Percent of respondents** | **Response** |
| --- | --- |
| 55% | –a task force or commission was established which still exists |
| 55% | –consciousness was raised |
| 18% | –hiring practices were affected; there are now more women in leadership roles |

(To this question, responses fell into more than one category.)

# Table 1. Women and Culture

**Maher 1974**

—the *demand of this technological age* for women to assume new and different positions and responsibilities (3)

—in their enthusiasm to *embrace and become part of the feminist claims* for recognition, some *women have adopted postures* which have done little to affirm the dignity of womanhood. (3)

—women's developing awareness of the unique personhood of human beings is *provoking them to dissatisfaction* with previously tolerated or accepted female roles and images (4)

—the [idealized] *image of woman denies woman her sovereign dignity* (6)

—the *falling away of traditional molds and criteria*, the stress and imperatives of our age, *impose the urgent necessity to enunciate again the pristine message* of the Gospel as related to women (6)

—philosophically attributed with elevated ideals, virtues and wisdom (Pr 8:22–31), *woman was reduced*—on the practical level—to the situation of a legal and social minor, discriminated against as a basic threat to man. (7)

—historically it is evident that *prejudice is passed from generation to generation, becoming enshrined in time as tradition and social custom*, seldom questioned and challenged. (9)

—the *effects of male dominance are embedded*, not only in custom and law, but most intrinsically in the psychological make-up of both men and women. (9)

—women's response to *the suggestiveness, immature appeal and insidious pressures of the communications and entertainment media* in their presentation of "feminine" models of behavior, thought and dress. (10)

—the *society in which we live could become wedded to and crippled by utilitarianism. If women should wed this spirit of our age, they may soon be widowed.* (10)

## Dozier 1975
—*the forces that place women upon the world stage and make "women" a live issue today in the international consciousness.* (1)
—*rejection and frustration heightened the demand* for rightful equality (1)
—*Where the assurance of law holds no promise,* it must be perceived that the *woman of today will find security in the global solidarity of her international sorority* (2)
—*woman's awakening is indeed as global as inflation* (3)
—For the woman, *the narrow institutions of the past seem more dispensable than ever, because woman has discovered her sister. Their mutual embrace reaches around the world; it is feminist, reverential, even ecclesial.* (3)
—*No woman is an island; every day she is being told: "You are a part of the mainland."* (3)
—Jesus Himself never once bowed to the cultural prejudices of his time that would have prohibited him from dealing with the woman of Samaria, Mary of Magdala . . . (4)
—*salted by the intransigence of religious tradition, spiced with Americana and the greater expectations of our cultural conditions, we hardly recognize the greater criteria for authenticity and honesty which have surfaced today.* (6)
—*the new age that is opening up* as women are increasingly allowed full participation in all sectors of society. (6)

## Buswell 1975
—the *underutilization of ethnic minority people and women* in decision-making and other official roles (1)

—(Jesus') *teachings as they related to women contradicted some of the most time-honored practices and prejudices* of the Jews (2)
—*As history unfolded,* the powerful of society became the powerful of the Church; the socially oppressed became the victims of racism and sexism within the Church. (2)
—We must *work together to reverse this trend and return to the early Christian ideal of true equality among all persons.* (2)

**Borders 1975**
—our *capacity to rise above the limitations* of human life (1)
—*the Church accepts what is good in all cultures. It tries to change those things which wound the lives of people,* becoming, as Jesus challenged us to be, *a leaven for society* (5)
—men and women of every age are *not only conditioned by a culture;* to a certain extent they are *prisoners of a culture* (5)
—Even though *in the past women have made their contributions in a man-centered world, their contributions in forming faith communities, while more subtle, in many areas have been more effective than the efforts of men.* (7)

**Minnesota Bishops 1977**
—neither society nor Church *can any longer tolerate the imposition of barriers in women's paths of growth* (6)
—*recognizing discrimination against women as contrary to God's intent* (6)
—*for too long, society has treated women in a cavalier fashion.* Guarded, protected, nurtured as if they were children . . . women have been guided only into the roles of mother, daughter, wife, sister, teacher. (8)
—*society's pattern for women is pre-set* (8)

—the American woman who works at home or as an unpaid volunteer suffers from *society's equation of money with status* . . . (9)
—*we decry the stereotyping of attributes* (10)
—*for too long women have been placed in positions of disproportionate opportunity and voice* (11)
—*the multidimensional problem of inequality* concerns us all (12)
—*equality needs to be nourished by new models of participation* (12)
—*as more and more women raise their own and society's consciousness of the dignity* of women, *a future of equality will be forged* (12)

**Minnesota 2**
—ours is a *culture which rightly stresses personhood, and persons cannot be so stereotyped, especially on the basis of sex, that they fit neatly into pre-ordained roles.* (15)
—women have a very *positive and constructive influence on society* (18)
—we recognize that women have frequently been *victims of injustice in many areas of the temporal order*—in culture and economics, in the trades and professions, in institutions of the political community. We condemn all unjust discrimination against them on the basis of sex. (18)
—*For their sex should never jeopardize their right to work and to equitable pay, to education, to housing, or to any other civil right in harmony with Christian values.* (18)
—We are concerned about those *women who suffer from society's tendency to dehumanize them by reducing them to mere objects or sources of pleasure, whether this is done with brazen openness . . . or . . . surreptitiously and covertly under some euphemistic guise.* (18–19)

### Hunthausen 1980
—none

### Gerety, 1981
—none

### Cummins 1981
—Many men and women see that *changes in our society call for a reassessment of women's capabilities.* (2)

### Balke and Lucker 1981
—*how counter Jesus went to the culture of his time* (4)

### Clark 1982
—we cannot try *to turn back the clock to a time* when today's questions did not exist (2)
—rape and violence against women are on the rise . . . graphic elements in the public consciousness (3)
—*a world speeding towards the twenty-first century poses questions* about the stability of marriage, the relationship between spouses, and responsibility to and for children. (4)
—changes in the Church and society *while opening new doors, also threaten cherished traditions* (21)
—danger that *poor women will be invisible to the vast majority* (44)
—*poor women are often inaudible . . . behind closed doors* (44)

### Weakland's Task Force Report 1982
—women were not encouraged to bond with other women, *for one binds oneself not to weakness but to strength.* Women have been socialized to *base their security in the self-assurance and good judgment of men* . . . in many cases women *derived their self-esteem from the approval* they received from men . . . this *situation has fostered a spirit of competition among women so*

that they vie with one another for men's attention, *not so much to win men as to find for themselves some sense of esteem and security.* (3A)

**Mahony 1987**
—*cultural stereotypes prevent honest communication* (1)

# Table 2. Women and the Church

**Maher 1974**
—*The liberation achieved by the Redemption establishes the recognition of the dignity and equality of woman before God, her right to full participation in the Church, and to reception of available sacramental graces.* (9)
—Endowed with God-given faith, hope and love, in the assurance of their identity and purpose, *women of the new world should indeed exert unprecedented power and influence to restore this universe to the state of peace and harmony cardinal to the divine plan for mankind.* (13)

**Dozier 1975**
—there is no doubt that *the universal woman is one of the great effective and credible transmitters of the Gospel. She goes into every nation beholding the presence of the Lord with her.* (4)
—*the liberated woman ... the most ready and apt media to energize and transmit the Gospel.* (4)
—Renewed awareness must continue and be followed by enthusiasm and the kind of *evangelical energy that provides the spiritual strength to lift the heart of humanity even higher where the reality of divine love will impress it.* (5)
—*Parish plants which once were the specific revelation of the Church's identity, concede to newer marks that are strangely feminine: welcome, friendship, love, hospitality, warmth. . . . This humanizing process leaves behind in history the scene of the representative clergy, who had all the answers and symbolized the Catholic Church for the immigrant thousands. It leaves behind the political types who refashioned parochial boundaries into political wards and stamped official ecclesial existence with the indelible mark of a male domain.* (5)

—There is a sinful condition of apathy and indifference in secular and church life. We find apathy among Christians when believers stop growing in maturity in Christ. Part of the reason might be, as far as woman is concerned, that the *woman no longer fits the traditional ecclesial role she inherited.* She is not enthusiastic about *a condition that has not kept pace with her life's experience.* She might even be depressed by the realization that no one really cares. *Yet the Church needs her gift, the Church needs the Christian woman in an ecclesial role that enriches her life and the life of her Church community with Christian vitality.* (6)

## Buswell 1975
—none

## Borders 1977
—Catherine and Teresa: *Despite these shining examples of a clear and visible role in the Church's life within the cultural patterns of the past, it is probably accurate to say that women have been rather silent members of the Church.* (7)
—However, *history recognizes that through their insight into Christ's presence and their dedication to His mission, they have made staggering contributions.* (7)
—*in today's society, if the Church is to continue as a force in the world, women must enter into decision and policy making,* and accept leadership roles within the Church. (8)
—*the further matter which inevitably enters any discussion* on the role of women in the Church: that of ordaining women to the priesthood. (10)
—N.B. I further note that *the recent document issued by the Sacred Congregation for the Doctrine of the Faith left open the possibility of admitting women to the diaconate. Through the Providence of God, the di-*

aconate was instituted to advance the mission of Christ in the service of the People of God. The Providence of God is still with us. (11)

## Minnesota 1 1979
—the voices of women . . . tell us that *the Church belongs in the forefront of Christian feminism* (6)
—Our pastoral concern goes out to all women in pain and alienation: to *the woman alienated from religion . . . the woman who hears God's call to serve through a variety of ministries or leadership positions but is blocked by tradition* (12)

## Minnesota 2
—women religious—*an intimate part of Church and society* (14)

## Hunthausen 1980
—Of Catherine of Siena: This laywoman and doctor of the church was known to have urged obedience to legal Church authority, while at the same time challenging popes *to face the structural issues of their day.* (1)
—we continue to *look critically at existing structures, to discern whether they foster or hinder full personhood of women and men in the Church.* (4)

## Gerety 1981
—the *church has been denied vast resources of talent in women* (7)
—the church's response to the challenge of the gospel imperative concerning the role of women *was at best ambiguous* (7)
—in our time *the church clearly desires* that women should become aware of the greatness of their mission and *take their equal, if sometimes different, place alongside their brothers in Christ.* (11)
—their [women's] role is of supreme importance . . . for

the rediscovery by believers of *the true face of the Church.* (11)

—*Let us understand with compassion the legitimate anger* on the part of some women *toward those structures or traditions which have demanded and expected less than full priesthood from them.* (2)

## Cummins 1981

—Women's *ministry is rooted in Baptism* where both men and women are given responsibility of ministry in the name of Christ, and in partnership becoming "one body . . . members of one another." (Rom 12:6) (2)

—throughout the Church's history, women have responded to the needs of their times. Pre-eminent was Mary . . . Teresa of Avila brought reform . . . Catherine of Siena *who rose to challenge divisions within the Church.* (2, 3)

## Balke and Lucker, 1981

—our primary interest: to exhort and encourage our local Churches and their parishes *to reflect today and tomorrow the attitudes of Jesus, our supreme model,* in their relationships with women in the Church. (10)

## Clark 1982

—I wish I could convey adequately in this letter *all the hidden and unsung goodness, strength and wisdom women have contributed to the Church* throughout all the years. (46)

—I directed that only ordained persons should preach the homily at the Eucharistic liturgy. My intention was then and is now *to be in concert with the whole college of bishops* . . . (66)

—We cannot ignore [women's] absence from advisory or decision-making bodies or positions; nor can we justify it on the grounds of their inexperience in certain kinds of Church affairs or their lack of certain skills. Such attempts at justification will create *a circle of self-*

*fulfilling prophecies* which will continue to keep many qualified women *at the periphery of Church affairs.* (88)

## Weakland 1982
—From Weakland's introduction: I beg all of you faithful *to see this report as getting to the heart* of one of the most important challenges facing the Church in our day.

## From Weakland's Task Force Report:
—*a change in theological vision . . . initiated a new age for women in the U.S. Catholic Church. Women listen keenly as the Church insists on the equality and dignity of all human persons. . . . The view of women as working for the Church is giving way to a new self-perception in which women view themselves as being the Church in service of others.* Where this perception has taken hold, women are assuming a sense of responsibility *for shaping the organization of the Church.* (see 3A)
—*Can the Church be a leader in society with regard to women or will the Church always follow society?* (3A)
—*How hard it is for many of us women to accept the dichotomy between the lip service paid to women's rights and the actual reality in the Church.* (3A)
—In many cases, it seems, *women are expected to make coffee while men make decisions. Women who do not abide by that expectation are frequently criticized by men and women alike.* (4A)
—Some women view the official Church as not only *lagging behind society . . .* but also as *failing its own vision* as expressed in the documents of Vatican II. (4A)

## Table 3. Women and Men

**Maher, 1974**

—*in the divine design,* men and women are meant to complement each other . . . (7)

—with the fall from grace, mankind *set their hearts against God* (Gen 6:5) and the *urge to attain and exert superiority over one another to dominate and subjugate came to possess all beings* (7)

—By nature of her biological processes, women's *activities were curtailed.* Pregnancy, child-bearing and rearing, *confined her to the environs of the living area. Man ranged afield unencumbered, engaged in the necessary business of hunting, fighting and establishing the boundaries of his domain.* (7)

—*in her circumscribed world,* a woman's work was largely individual and of limited authority. *Man, on the other hand, was perforce drawn into group action, wars and protective councils* . . . (7)

—the female biological experience, misunderstood by primitive males, evoked *anxiety and a superstitious fear which militated against women.* (7)

—*Immeasurable potential may be lost to the Church and society by too rigidly exclusive male and female roles. The traditionally opposite yet complementary trends of protector (male) and nurturer (female) must be reconciled if mankind is to realize its identity as the image of God*—God, who is both protector and nurturer, strong and gentle, forgiving and accepting, loving and giving, and who allows complete freedom of will. (11)

**Dozier 1975**

—Neither men nor women will come to full personhood in *a society where the gifts of one or the other are suppressed. "Male and female, God created them," and their complementary interaction and development brings each to maturity.* (6)

## Buswell 1975
—none

## Borders 1977
—*men and women of every age are not only conditioned by a culture; to a certain extent they are prisoners of a culture* (4)

## Minnesota 1, 1979
—The task before us is *how to bring that day nearer when full partnership will be a reality* and when inevitable sacrifices will be shared together. (12)

## Minnesota 2, 1979
—the differences *beyond the merely biological . . . are intrinsic to God's basic purpose in creation, for man and woman in close partnership* were given the responsibility to beget and to rear children and *to exercise authority, in God's stead,* over all the rest of creation. (15)
—*Arising out of these differences come certain principles* which affect the relationships between women and men. One of the most important of these is that of complementarity. . . . *This notion shall be an underlying principle* in these reflections. (15)
—We believe that (self-fulfillment and emotional fulfillment of their children) will happen *if they maintain that clear complementarity* between them which involves their whole being and *flows from the fact that "male and female he created them." (Gen. 1 and 2).* (16)
—such *clear complementarity not only enriches and strengthens their marital union and partnership,* but also enables children to mature with an *accurate image* of woman as wife and mother and man as husband and father. (16)
—We are compelled, however, to mention our distrust of *those feminist movements which seem either to ignore the God-given differences* between women and

men or *to equate indiscriminately the values of a career with those of a home*. For it seems to us that such movements *attempt to masculinize women and to put them in unhealthy competition, if not in outright contention, with men*. Such attempts, we believe, are harmful to womanhood, to family life, to society and to the Church. (19)

## Hunthausen 1980
—Solidarity marks the sexes (2)
—*Sexual love* (in the Song of Songs) *expands existence beyond the stereotypes of society*—no male dominance, no female subordination, no stereotyping of either sex. (2)

## Gerety 1981
—*As partners in the mission* of Christ, men and women are called to a ministry of shared responsibility, where the special gifts, talents and competencies of each are *harmoniously activated in complementarity and mutuality.* (9)

## Cummins 1981
—none

## Balke and Lucker 1981
—For women, *the psychological costs of sexism are indeed extremely high: the tendency toward psychological paralysis, disabling them from asserting their self-worth. For men, the costs of sexism are also high: they are victimized by hyper-rationalism, by an underdeveloped affective life, by the need to dominate and control.* (3)

## Clark 1982
—none

## Weakland's Task Force Report 1982
—From Weakland's introduction:
—*We are being asked to stretch our horizons a bit. We*

*are being asked to let go of stereotypes. We are being asked to search out what following Christ together as men and women really means.* (1)

**Mahony 1987**
—*We need to recover a greater sense of men and women working collaboratively, side by side.* (3)
—*Women . . . wish to join with men as partners in the task of working to bring about the Kingdom of justice and peace. . . .* (2)

## Table 4. Conversion and Reconciliation

**Maher 1974**
—*If inequities are not to be exacerbated,* but freely acknowledged and eradicated, *the human possessiveness and pride which dominates so much of human relationships must be replaced with genuine religious charity.* (12)
—In truly religious faith, *women will find liberation from the social, legal and cultural absurdities which disrupt the harmony of human existence.* In religious hope, they may *transcend the pressures of moral and social decline.* (13)
—*The sensate culture of our age dwarfs human growth and fragments our lives.* It is our hope that *women of the new world may take the initiative to restore and rebuild our culture to that wholistic conformation which will bring mankind to the fullness of life—a culture to bridge the gap between human beings and between the human and the divine.* (3)

**Dozier 1975**
—Not even the prophets of the sixties foresaw how *deeply centered in the Christian mystery the movement for equality for women ought to be.* (1)
—Renewed awareness must continue and be followed by enthusiasm and *the kind of evangelical energy that provides the spiritual strength to lift the heart of humanity even higher where the reality of divine love will impress it.* (5)

**Buswell 1975**
—We must *work together to reverse this trend* (of racism and sexism within the Church) and *return to the early Christian ideal of true equality* among all persons. (2)
—I ask your help in *developing a concrete, affirmative plan for eliminating the injustice of discrimination in every parish and other diocesan unit* . . . (4) Nineteen

hundred and seventy-five, proclaimed by the United Nations as International Women's Year, *is a fitting time to begin.* (4)

## Borders 1977
—*our future as a Church is in the hands of God's providence* (4)
—*the Church must grow and therefore change* (4)

## Minnesota 1, 1979
—*As more and more women raise their own and society's consciousness of the dignity of women, a future of equality will be forged.* (12)
—*If we close our ears and minds, we ignore half of the people of God. If we listen to our sisters' voices with open minds and hearts, the benefits to our society will be multiple.* (12)

## Minnesota 2, 1979
—We encourage women, working within the context of the teachings of the Church and her Lord, *to accept the challenge of righting the wrongs we have alluded to, and others besides.* (19)
—*We look forward to the day when women will receive not mere privilege which may be taken away with impunity, but that full justice which cannot be denied them without violating the Gospel.* (19)

## Hunthausen 1980
—*Conversion is the process each must undergo in becoming the new person through faith and baptism. A new version of Church, a renewed sense of mission and community, impel each and every person to inquire: what does a Church look like that is whole, just, and moving toward full incarnation of the Kingdom?* (3)

**Gerety 1981**
—Today, as responsible Christians, *we must face the injustices we see with a mind toward eradicating them* in that continuing process of conversion that will never end until the completion of all things in Christ. (2)
—*The Church should be a model of what the human community is meant to be and can be under the Gospel.* (2)
—As we preach Christ to the world, *we must undergo conversion and put our own household of faith in order.* (2)
—I call upon all in responsible positions to give particular attention to *the speedy integration of women into all the various structures and ministries,* and to open to them all the developing opportunities for service *as we move toward continuing spiritual renewal, reconciliation and evangelization.* (12)
—All of us . . . should translate our Christian principles of justice into action in our free American society by *vigorously supporting legislation to correct inequality based on sex in employment, education, business, housing, welfare and family support.* (12)
—I urge all our priests, religious and lay people *to do all in their power to eliminate all vestiges of un-Christian discrimination* between men and women. (12)

**Cummins 1981**
—none

**Balke and Lucker 1981**
—This pastoral . . . is written in the hope that *it will raise to a new level of awareness the issue of Christian feminism and the sin of sexism.* (2)
—The purpose of (the) examination of conscience is *to raise our consciousness on issues related to Chris-*

*tian feminism, not to create guilt feelings. We offer it as an aid to determine our attitudes and practices in the Church toward women, and as a checklist for moving towards a more thorough acceptance* of women into the life of the local Church both on the diocesan and the parish levels. (12)

**Clark 1982**
—Through prayer, reflection and genuine action inspired by new insights, our goal is to realize as Church that profound reconciliation of men and women *for which Christ hungers and of which he is the means.* (22)
—In my judgment, we need constantly *to reform attitudes and practices among us which fall short of recognizing the full dignity and stature of every person.* (29)

**Weakland's Task Force Report 1982**
From Weakland's introduction:
—Most of all the (listening) process must be one of reconciliation; *we are not involved in a contest nor in a debate.* (1)
—*We are being asked to stretch our horizons a bit. We are being asked to let go of stereotypes. We are being asked to search out what following Christ together as men and women really means.* (1)

From the Task Force Report:
—Recommend that . . . the Church of Southeast Wisconsin . . . *undertake concrete and visible efforts to seek reconciliation with women who suffer the effects of sexist attitudes and practices within the Church.* (12A)
—*Women are standing up straight.* As this happens, some are indignant; many rejoice. We perceive this as the continuing challenge. It is *our hope that the entire Church be energized by the search of women for wholeness and reconciliation. We believe that in this*

*process, gender will shed its evil association with division and become what it was meant to be—a sacrament of unity, reconciliation, and wholeness.* (12A)

## Mahony 1987

—Such a service [of reconciliation] could be *a privileged moment* here within our Archdiocese in the *ongoing conversion to new ways of relating to one another* as women and men in the Church, *as members of the same family.* (4)

—This [process of reconciliation] *will require a painful dying to self for us all.* (4)